# Cannizzaro: Beyond th

## Tony Matthews

WSMP

Cannizaro, Beyond the Gates
by Tony Matthews

Published by Wimbledon Society Museum Press, an imprint of AAPPL, Artists' and Photographers' Press Ltd., Church Farm House, Wisley, Surrey, GU23 6QL
info@aappl.com    www.wimbledonmuseum.org.uk
in co-operation with Friends of Cannizaro Park, c/o Willow House, 35 High Street, Wimbledon Village, London SW19 5BY    www.cannizaropark.org.uk

Sales and distribution: contact AAPPL info@aappl.com or visit the
Wimbledon Society Museum of Local History, open 2.30 – 5.00 pm on Saturdays and Sundays at 22 Ridgway, SW19 4QN or go to the museum's website www.wimbledonmuseum.org.uk to purchase online
Copyright © AAPPL 2010
Illustrations: © Tony Matthews, Paul Bonner, Martin Newth, Dennis Robbins, Nancy-Joan & Peter Seligman, Andy McIlvenna, and the organisers of the Cannizaro Park Open Air Festival. Others courtesy of Wimbledon Society Museum of Local History.
Portrait of the Duchess of Cannizaro (p 9) from the National Portrait Gallery
Portrait of Cdre George Johnstone (p 29) from National Galleries of Scotland
American Red Cross Hospital (p 40) courtesy of the National Museum of Health and Medicine, Washington DC, USA
Text © Tony Matthews 2010

All rights reserved. No part of this publication may be reproduced, stored in a retrieval system, copied, or transmitted in any form or by any means, electronic, mechanical, photocopying, recording or otherwise without the prior written permission of the copyright owner.
A catalogue record for this book is available from the British Library.

ISBN 9781904332978
Design, contents: Tony Matthews & Cameron Brown
Design, cover: Cameron Brown    Set in Times TT
Printed and bound in Great Britain by Intype Libra Limited, Wimbledon, www.intypelibra.co.uk
Front cover: *Diana and the Fawn* Title page: *Cannizaro Gates* by Eveline Hastings

# Contents                                Page

Foreword                                        5
Chapter 1: Introduction                         7
Chapter 2: Why the name?                       12
Chapter 3: Three centuries                     31
Chapter 4: Going public                        49
Chapter 5: Municipal revival                   56
Chapter 6: Art shows and festival fun          64
Chapter 7: Keeping the magic alive             81
Chapter 8: The future                         102
Trees to look for                             104
Occupants of Cannizaro House                  106
Index                                         107
Acknowledgements                              111

*Black Pine (Pinus nigra), Mediterranean Garden*

# Foreword

This is not the first published work about the 34 very special acres of Cannizaro Park and the house of the same name beside Wimbledon Common. Other writers have mentioned their colourful residents over the first 250 years and the gardens' fine landscaping with rare shrubs and trees, mostly planted in more recent times. But no earlier book has told the complete story, linking history and horticulture to art, entertainment, and recent battles to preserve the magic of this precious enclave in south-west London.

Since 1987, Cannizaro House Hotel has invited clientele to a romantic setting largely dependent on the beautiful scenery beyond its doors. From 1989-2008, the annual open air festival saw successive organisers struggling against financial odds to continue Cannizaro's long musical and dramatic tradition. As a venue for visual arts too its beauty draws back exhibitors year after year.

Cannizaro is a rare treasure among parks. This was recognised by the Borough of Merton when it was registered as an English Heritage Grade II* garden in October 1987, one of very few in Greater London. It held the status of a flagship park and its bedding displays were used to promote Merton as a whole - a proud alternative to Wimbledon's All-England Lawn Tennis Club down the hill.

Circumstances change. Merton's top funding priorities no longer include Cannizaro and its future cannot be taken for granted. But for those who know and love its grounds, it remains a magical retreat. The story continues.

*Fresh azaleas, Lady Jane's Wood*

# Chapter 1: Introduction

Cannizaro Park, Wimbledon, first opened free of charge to a post-war weary general public on Saturday 2$^{nd}$ April 1949. At a ceremony attended by local officials and the mayors of neighbouring boroughs, Wimbledon's own mayor, Alderman W E Hamlin, said he doubted whether any other public park so close to London could combine such natural beauty with a unique collection of unusual trees and shrubs.

It was a proud day for the local community. The weekend was marked by an art exhibition in the now publicly owned Cannizaro House and the opening ceremony, complete with the planting of a new magnolia tree beside the Sunken Garden, was filmed by a local cine club.

The new public park reflected a national consensus about the value of municipal gardens to Britain's urban communities. This dated back more than a century. In 1833, Parliament's Select Committee on Public Works had reported the health benefits of providing "lungs for the city". By the 1840s, general access to urban parkland featured strongly among early Victorian measures to improve living conditions for London's rapidly growing population. Two nearby royal palaces, Hampton Court and Kew, were among many previously exclusive locations whose gardens had opened as public pleasure grounds.

In the 100 years prior to its opening, members of the general public had entered the grounds of Cannizaro on many occasions but only by special invitation. Part of the grounds had recently been made available for allotments during the Second World War and other people invited through the gates had included girl guides attending jamborees or collecting firewood for distribution to the poor. But such access had only begun to happen comparatively recently.

Writing of his childhood memories before the First World War, local resident Patrick Fawcett said of Cannizaro: "The house and grounds were beautifully kept but the gates were always closed and we saw no sign of life."[1] Anyone had been able to explore Wimbledon Common long before its legal protection in 1871, but there was no question of uncontrolled entry to the large walled

estate to its south-west, any more than to any other large private garden.
The estate got its name from two of its earlier tenants, the Duke and Duchess of Cannizzaro who lived there intermittently from 1817 until 1841. After their deaths in that year, the lease on both the house and nearly 60 acres of grounds was taken up by a series of equally exclusive tenants and the property was to stay in private hands for another 107 years.

*Satirical views of the Duke of Cannizzaro dancing at Almack's in 1815 (centre profile above) and the Duchess around 1830 in her prime (opposite) by Sir Edwin Landseer*

Nevertheless, the "upstairs, downstairs" society of the day meant that both of Benjamin Disraeli's two nations[2] – the rich and the poor – were well represented. While the leaseholders passed a leisured existence amid genteel society and well manicured scenery, they were outnumbered by domestic and gardening staff, many living in cottages on the estate.

In the 1860s the Boustead family, a couple and their six children, had more than 20 servants including six gardeners, three kitchen staff, three in the laundry, three housemaids, a governess, butler, lady's maid, footman, carpenter, coachman and stable-hand. They were joined by five horses and two dogs. To accommodate them all, the lease cost £300 a year.

Whatever passed in the lives of these people, the grounds of Cannizaro were always a peaceful and beautiful retreat, comfortably distant from what was then the world's largest metropolis, London, with its crowded and dirty streets and perpetual pollution.

Cannizaro sat upon an undulating landscape overlooking the Surrey Downs. In prehistoric times it had formed a small part of an extensive swampland beside the River Thames. This had dried out to leave the thousands of acres

of what are now Wimbledon and Putney Commons and Richmond Park with gravel subsoil and acid topsoil unsuited to arable farming. It was eventually colonised by woodland, particularly oak and silver birch, and this in turn had partly given way to grazing and pasture land by the 18th century.

From its creation in the early 1700s until the early 20th century, residents of what became the Cannizaro estate had access to a much bigger area than today's 34 acres of municipal park. There were gardens, meadows and woods, and without leaving their own property they could wander as far as Wimbledon Wood, bordering Copse Hill. Nothing obstructed their path towards Warren Farm and the view was clear as far as Coombe Hill on the way to Kingston.

Today the area west and south of Cannizaro Park is largely covered by houses, roads and, since 1907, the Royal Wimbledon Golf Course. Where traffic on the A3 now provides permanent if distant background noise, residents then heard only the sounds of rural life – grazing cattle and sheep, the occasional clatter of farm vehicles, the clip-clop of horses, and the constant variation of birdsong and the elements. Occasionally the tranquillity would have been broken by gunfire during the shooting season or rifle training on the Common. Otherwise disturbance was minimal.

Cannizaro Park today is very different, of course, but apart from brief interruptions by occasional open air festivals or other special events, it is still usually quiet and relaxing. This tranquillity is far more precious in our world of 24-hour communications and entertainment, traffic jams and suburban noise. Outside the park gates, a still pleasant but now distinctly un-rural village lies a few minutes walk away, with Wimbledon town a little further down the hill. Parking and construction works often reduce surrounding road widths to those of old country lanes but that doesn't stop traffic from racing past the park on Common West Side if given the chance. Historic local taverns are as busy as ever but now face competition from cosmopolitan restaurants and coffee shops in the village. Aircraft overhead testify to the the expansion of Heathrow flight paths and fairground sound systems on the Common provide yet another example of constantly rising noise. Even the ice cream van has its bell.

Year-round, Cannizaro Park sits amidst all of this, a place of escape where the pace of life reverts from a race to a crawl. Of course, it is not an isolated green space. The Common is just across the road and Wimbledon still has plenty of other greenery with metropolitan open land and public parks providing some refuge from every day stress. Indeed, south-west London as a whole retains more protected woodland and heathland than the rest of the capital. Add the even bigger area accounted for by private gardens and the picture looks comparatively good for nature lovers.

But Cannizaro's landscaping and botanical attractions offer a very particular experience of the great outdoors. Few other locations have anything like the range of trees and plants from so many other parts of the world as well as the indigenous species so familiar elsewhere. This is Wimbledon's answer to the Royal Botanical Gardens, a comparison made by none other than the Curator of Kew himself when Cannizaro stood on the verge of public ownership before Alderman Hamlin's big day over 60 years ago.[3]

Moreover, the year-round colour, scents and spectacular blooms of Cannizaro Park are complemented by artworks, some transient, some permanent, but all capable of stimulating thought and emotion. It is a magical place. This book tells of its past and present. The priority now is its future.

# NOTES

1: *Memories of a Wimbledon Childhood* 1906-1918, Patrick Fawcett, 1981.
2: "I was told that the Privileged and the People formed Two Nations", *Sybil*, Benjamin Disraeli, 1845.
3: *Merton & Morden News*, 8th April 1949.

# Chapter 2: Why the name?

The obvious question everyone asks about Cannizaro is why the Italian name? It certainly intrigued the local people of Wimbledon when they first heard it in the early 19th century.

It dates back to August 1829 when the official resident of what was then Warren House, a large mansion beside the Common, secured the Sicilian title, Duke of Cannizzaro. The lucky man was Francis Platamone, Count St Antonio, leaseholder of Warren House since 1817 thanks to his wealthy heiress wife, Sophia.

This was their country retreat in Surrey. Their main home was 20 Hanover Square in central London, where they owned the freehold. They had a house in Brighton too. But for nearly a quarter of a century, the bucolic Wimbledon house and its parkland provided a setting for their disastrous marriage. Francis undoubtedly got more out of the pairing than Sophia but each contributed to a story that would preoccupy the gossip and scandal-mongers for the best part of three decades.

So who exactly were this exotic Italian immigrant and his wife and why did they choose to live in Wimbledon? To start with the Duke.

**From wildness to refinement**

Francis Platamone, Count St Antonio, was born in 1784, one of three children of Baldassarre Platamone, Duke of Cannizzaro, a spot near the Sicilian town of Catania.[1] They lived in Palermo, provincial capital within the Kingdom of the Two Sicilies. The family apparently originated in Spain but had been important on the island since the 16th century. Francis' brother Michele, Prince Ludica, was a year older and their sister Concetta, the Contessa Platamone, Princess St Cataldo, was younger. They had a string of other titles too.

They were a wild family. Their father squandered his wealth on riotous living and the sons followed suit. Only their mother Rosalia, Princess Ladaria, was restrained, charitable and religious. In 1799, they were joined by a slightly older French youth, Eugene de Mazenod, acting as a mentor. A future Bishop of Marseilles who would one day be sanctified, he was a restraining influence on a family he later described as "an inexhaustible source of madness".

He stayed for three years. Then in 1802 Rosalia died suddenly, Eugene was heartbroken and left, and the brothers became uncontrollable. Michele married a local princess but continued chasing women and was eventually locked up in a monastery as punishment. He emerged somewhat chastened and got a post at the royal court in Naples. Francis joined the palace guard, the Royal Grenadiers, but is said to have "plunged into an evil life".

Both Michele and Concetta were to survive Francis as they are mentioned in his last will and testament.[2] In later years Michele had a young son, also called Baldassarre, who died in 1849. He himself died in 1858. All the Platamone titles then passed to the Galletti family of Concetta's husband.

Back to Francis. How it came about is unclear but by 1813 he had come to London, representing the Sicilian monarchy in some role at the Court of St James. He is first mentioned at the Prince Regent's levee at Carlton House and mixed in the highest of social circles, eventually becoming a naturalised British citizen. He is described by the contemporary diarist Charles Greville as "a good looking, intelligent but penniless Sicilian of high birth who was pretty successful in all ways in society".[3]

At that time, British court society took its lead from the Prince Regent, the future King George IV, and social acceptability depended upon a combination of family history and evident wealth. Those who boasted both impressive aristocratic antecedents and plenty of money were well placed to reinforce their status through advantageous marriages. If, like the Count St Antonio, you had little wealth but could boast a pedigree and match it with charm, you stood a reasonable chance of success. But wealth alone was insufficient to bring respect. The upper, not the middle classes, ruled the roost. The rest of the population didn't count at all.

A test of quality was success at the fashionable Almack's Assembly Room in London. This is described by another contemporary diarist, the Duchess of Dino, as "an institution where young ladies find husbands, women of position an exercising ground for their pretensions, novelists the most brilliant scenes in their stories, foreigners their introduction to society, and everybody a more or less legitimate interest to occupy them in the height of the season".[4]

To obtain sponsored entry to Almack's and impress the influential at its many balls and social engagements was a distinct advantage to anyone with high society ambitions. No easy matter, however. The Duchess of Dino called it "the despair of the middle classes, the object of the emulation and desire of so many young ladies in the provinces, Almack's which gives or withholds the stamp of fashion, Almack's the despotism par excellence, ruled with a rod of iron by six of the most exclusive ladies in London".

Breeding and charm alone helped Francis Platamone to pass the Almack's test. In June 1814 he married the heiress Sophia Johnstone, setting up house in Hanover Square near her mother's home. According to *The Times*, Sophia was "a beautiful heiress, daughter of a celebrated pin-maker, who bequeathed to her an immense fortune". However, Greville describes her as "very short and fat with rather a handsome face, totally uneducated but full of humour, vivacity and natural drollery, at the same time passionate and capricious". Her caricature in the National Portrait Gallery (see page 9) suggests the latter was probably closer to the mark.

The couple maintained a very active life within high society but regardless of the marriage, the Count St Antonio continued his reputation as a dance partner at Almack's. An engraving dated 1815 (see page 8) shows him dancing with Princess Esterhazy, wife of the Austrian Ambassador, while Beau Brummell, fashion-setter of the day, converses with the Duchess of Rutland. Count St Aldiconde, watches nearby.[5]

Italian expatriates were particularly noticeable in English high society gossip at that time. Most notorious was Bartolommeo Bergami, chamberlain to and lover of the Princess of Wales. Their relationship led to divorce proceedings, enforced exile, and her rejection as Queen when the Prince Regent succeeded to the throne in 1820. Francis Platamone, future Duke of Cannizzaro, didn't reach quite such dizzy heights but he does seem to have held his own in the circles that mattered.

**Living in Wimbledon**

On 30th September 1815, Sophia gave birth to their only child, George Wellington Francis Balthasar Saint Antonio. Sadly he didn't live long enough to make his own mark on the world but at least his names represented both families well enough. "George" was in the Johnstone family tradition, "Wellington" the hero of the day, and the rest pure Cannizzaro. He died less than two years later on 17th May 1817 and was buried in Westminster Abbey alongside Sophia's late brother.

Wimbledon, a peaceful rural retreat, offered a much needed bolt-hole from the rigours of London, so Francis and Sophia sought consolation there, leasing Warren House in the same year. The Surrey village had long been a favourite of the rich and famous so there would have been no shortage of social possibilities, even if it seemed a little slow compared to the capital. The Count became a voluntary, if irregular, subscriber to the local evening lectures given by Rev H Lindsay.

Sophia, on the other hand, was passionate about music. On 24th March 1817, not long before their little son's death, she hosted a grand musical party at Hanover Square. It set a precedent for what would also become a tradition of recitals or concerts at the house in Wimbledon, one that would not only survive Sophia herself but be revived by later residents and echoed nearly 200 years later in the annual Cannizaro Park festival. With its own library of musical manuscripts, the beautiful setting of Warren House became a centre for musical entertainment, if only for select circles in those days.

But for all its romantic setting, Wimbledon did nothing to change an irredeemably tempestuous marriage. Greville says the Count was "disgusted" by his wife and for most of the following 24 years from 1817, only one or other of the couple actually lived at Warren House. For some years they shared a place in society, hosting spectacular parties for distinguished guests yet the marriage actually survived in name only for the rest of their lives. The poor rate book for 1831 records the house in Sophia's name, the highways rate book for 1833 records the Duke, while the poor rate book for 1838 reverts to Sophia.[6]

## The Johnstone legacy

Sophia's family history is much better documented than that of her husband. She was the illegitimate daughter of a highly controversial figure with countless enemies and a dodgy private life. It may explain Sophia's ultimate refusal to be defeated either by her outrageous husband or gossip-mongers.

Sophia's father was Commodore George Johnstone MP, director of the East India Company and former Governor of West Florida, who fathered several children by a woman far younger than himself, maintained them as a family at Hanover Square, but then married someone else simply to secure a title for legitimate offspring. This was the sort of thing that members of the royal family (although not the very loyal King George III himself) got away with but it raised eyebrows among respectable lesser mortals. To cap it all, the marriage proved a miserable and loveless mismatch.

Born in 1730, fourth son of Sir James Johnstone, the 3rd Baronet of Westerhall, Dumfries, George Johnstone joined the Merchant Navy before switching to the Royal Navy in 1746. Shortly after his promotion to lieutenant in 1755, he faced a court martial for "insubordination and disobedience". However, his record of gallantry in combat was taken into account and he was merely reprimanded in 1757. He was promoted Captain Johnstone in 1762 and secured the rank of commodore the following year.

In November 1763 he was appointed Governor of the British colony of West Florida, newly taken from the French. He held the post for four years while British settlers established a community that would remain loyal to the Crown during the American War of Independence a few years later.

His private life was less exemplary. He was "naturally of an amourous complexion"[7] and while still a lieutenant, established what would become a lifelong relationship with Martha Ford, an actress, whom he "debauched... when quite a child". Despite this, she was said to be "a very respectable, accomplished and witty woman who conducted herself in the most irreproachable manner". Their eldest son John was born around 1760 but drowned aged 20 during a hurricane off the coast of St Lucia. They had three more sons, George Lindsay, James Primrose and Alexander Patrick, and one daughter, Sophia. Born in 1785, she would become Duchess of Cannizzaro nearly 45 years later.

Commodore Johnstone returned to Britain in 1767 and gained a series of seats in Parliament as an Independent for the next 20 years, becoming notorious for "his shameless and scurrilous utterances".[8] In December 1770, after publicly insulting the Colonial Secretary, Lord George Sackville-Germain, for "cowardice in battle", he fought an inconclusive duel rather than apologise.

He was a member of the Carlisle Peace Commission during the American War of Independence but the colonists refused to negotiate with him in 1778, accusing him of bribery. Loyal to the Crown, he was given command of a naval squadron off the coast of Portugal in 1779 and won a battle against the French, allies of the Americans. It made no difference. Britain lost the war anyway and the United States was born, later absorbing Johnstone's former colony in Florida.

In 1782 at the age of 52 and despite repeated promises of marriage to Martha, he married Charlotte Dee, daughter of the vice-consul in Lisbon, aged just 20. He was keen to return to England immediately after the wedding but his "handsome" and "dashing" new bride was strong willed and refused to leave Lisbon for weeks afterwards. It was not a good start.

However, she did produce a legitimate son, John Lowther Johnstone (1783-1811), who would succeed George's older brother, William Johnstone Pulteney as 5th Baronet of Westerhall. But this was the only benefit of his betrayal of Martha. Charlotte was said to be "a tartar" for his remaining years, adding to his self-inflicted misery. Had he lived, he would have been little cheered to see the baronetcy title lapse anyway with John Lowther's death aged just 28.

In 1783 George Johnstone became a director of the East India Company where he was soon notorious for obstructing disciplinary action against his brother, a retired nabob, over exploitation of Indians. He became an enemy of politician Henry Dundas, a powerful voice on the Board of Control for India who also happened to be resident at Warren House, Wimbledon, at the time. Of course, George could never have imagined the future enduring link between his own daughter and the same house.

He spent his last years engaged in legal battles over lost prize money from a confiscated Dutch ship and personal wrangling with a former subordinate. Beset by crises on all sides, he was forced to resign in 1785, suffered from Hodgkin's disease, and died in May 1787. According to his biographer, Johnstone's career "demonstrated how the 18th century system, connection ridden racket that it was, enabled a man to rise to heights where he had no business to be".

**Aunt Sophia and the Johnstone clan**

Such were Sophia's antecedents, unpromising perhaps but certainly not in the matter of money. The future Duchess of Cannizzaro was just two years old when her father, Commodore Johnstone, died. She and her three surviving older brothers are listed in his will of May 1786 and he supported them all, alongside Martha. (He also left £500 a year to Charlotte who then married a future admiral, outranking Johnstone - a final insult beyond the grave.)

As a youngster, Sophia established quite a reputation in the Prince Regent's social circle alongside her favourite brother, George Lindsay (1767-1813). They hosted a particularly memorable ball in 1805, going to some lengths to ensure the Prince and his mistress, Mrs Fitzherbert, could both attend. Unfortunately the whole event was ruined, coming the very day after news arrived of Lord Nelson's death at Trafalgar. The two top guests failed to materialise but the ball carried on regardless. Sophia's social ambitions were boundless and could not be undermined by the inconvenient death of England's greatest hero of the day. [9]

George Lindsay - sometimes known as Johnstone Jnr - became an MP like his father and prospered as assistant to the British resident at Lucknow, India. However, he did not match the commodore's career. Leading a pretty dissolute life as a profligate gambler, he never married but did father two daughters. He was said to be "touched by madness" in his final years. Sophia is thought to have helped care for him before he died of a stroke at the age of 46. He was buried in the south cloister of Westminster Abbey, joined four years later by his nephew and namesake, Sophia's infant son, the child who might also have become Duke of Cannizzaro had he lived.

Her other two brothers, James Primrose and Alexander Patrick, had both died young while in India. Alexander had married one Maria d'Aguilar and produced a son, George Bueller, and two daughters, Emily and Sophia Augusta. (They may have been twins, a recurrent feature of the Johnstone family.) Alexander also worked for the East India Company but he died in 1803 and the following year his widow Maria and the three children all returned to England.

The deaths of both George Lindsay and two years earlier her half brother, John Lowther the Baronet, left Sophia inheriting a fortune by 1813. Years later in 1831 when her mother Martha also died aged 86, she inherited a further £30,000 (many millions in today's values) plus an annuity of £1000. Sophia's nieces would become familiar faces at her various homes including Wimbledon. Her marriage to the Count St Antonio in 1814 may not have provided wedded bliss but it did confer an immediate title that proved highly useful for her role as a high society hostess. Later elevation to the status of Duchess of Cannizzaro would reinforce this.

So too the presence of attractive young nieces. When on 16th April 1820, Baron Philip von Neumann, the Austrian charge d'affaires and friend of Ambassador Prince Esterhazy, dined with the Count and Countess, he fell head over heels in love with the late Alexander's 17-year-old daughter Emily as they all listened to the excellent musical entertainment.[10] The visit was the first of many he would make to the future Duke and Duchess of Cannizzaro, usually on separate occasions when they were apart.

A month later on 19th May, von Neumann had another delightful encounter with Emily and her sister as they sang together. He afterwards described her as "a finished beauty" who gave one "an idea of Rebecca in Scott's novel". How good the singing really was remains unclear but he admits in his diary that he did not know a note of music - "which proves that boldness comes to one's help when talent is absent".

*The Morning Chronicle* of 7th June mentions the Baron at a concert of vocal and instrumental music in the Great Saloon of the Count and Countess St Antonio's Hanover Square house when the Opera Corps and the Demoizelles de Lihu were present. The Esterhazys were there too, together with Prince Lichtenstein, Prince Francaville, Prince Sapicha, Earl of Glengale, the Viscount and Viscountess Granville. On 9th July von Neumann was back at Warren House and delighted to see Emily, her sister and mother. Things were becoming serious. He wrote in his diary that he was thinking of marrying her, adding: "She is an amiable, charming creature and appears to possess all that is necessary for domestic happiness."

A few days later on 13th July while at a reception at the Duke of Devonshire's home he "was bored because I was unable to get near her on whom my thoughts are now centred". But he listened carefully when Count Lieven, another influential figure of the day, told him that "the three leading men in the state, the Archbishop of Canterbury, the Lord Chancellor and the Lord Privy Seal, had all run away with their wives".

He and Emily apparently became engaged to be married. Whether Sophia, Countess St Antonio, was aware of this is unclear but she would doubtless have been pleased. On 28th July the Baron accompanied Emily and her sister to the fashionable Vauxhall Pleasure Gardens. But what happened next is a mystery.

There is no record of what Emily herself thought and all went quiet in August. The Baron makes no mention of her when meeting the Count and Countess St Antonio at Greenwich on 4th September, or when he and Princess Esterhazy visited Sophia alone in Wimbledon on 21st October. That same evening he headed off to Covent Garden to watch a performance of Shakespeare's "Henry IV" without a word about "the amiable and charming creature".

The relationship obviously fizzled out. Baron von Neumann went on to others but remained a confirmed bachelor until marrying the Duke of Beaufort's daughter many years later in 1844. It did not affect his friendship with the future Cannizzaros as he remained on good terms with them both as their marriage crumbled.

As for the "finished beauty", Emily, and her sister Sophia Augusta, whatever romances they did have never bore fruit. Both were still spinsters over 20 years later when the Duke and Duchess of Cannizzaro died within months of each other in England and Italy respectively.

**Glittering society, marital failure**

Neither their son's death in 1817 nor their fiery relationship stopped the Count and Countess St Antonio from demonstrating their wealth and status to society. In May 1819, the year before Baron von Neumann appeared on the scene, they had entertained the Duke and Duchess of Wellington, Count and Countess Lieven and other distinguished guests at Hanover Square, followed by a grand concert for 300 people, Sophia's second musical event.

"Four magnificent drawing rooms were thrown open and most brilliantly illuminated," reported the *Morning Chronicle*. The Prince Regent, soon to become King George IV, was among their guests and in turn, the Count was among those attending the Prince's grand fancy dress ball at Carlton House. Having the house in fashionable Brighton was also useful. In July 1821 *The Times* reported the Count and Countess respectively as steward and patroness of a grand coronation fete there for the new monarch. The pair were seen together at music festivals elsewhere in the country and they clearly cultivated their royal connections, hosting the Duke of Cambridge, the King's younger brother, at Wimbledon in 1822.

Francis did not hesitate to use his wife's money to prosper in business as well as social circles. He was on the Committee of Noblemen running the King's Theatre (today Her Majesty's) in the Haymarket and his other endeavours included a directorship of the South American Association for Agricultural and Other Objects, and a management role of the Royal Academic Concerts.

He also made the news pages for appearances in the courts of justice. In 1824 he successfully defended a footman who had been arrested during a disturbance in Hanover Square involving servants.[11] The following year he was himself summonsed to appear before magistrates over non-payment of the poor rate.

In 1825 the press reported his plans to develop a new square in Brighton with a large new house at its centre. *The Morning Chronicle* reported: "The greatest sensation was produced on Saturday by the sale of a single acre of ground, divided into 15 lots, on the West Cliff at Brighton, the property of the Count and Countess St Antonio. The 15 lots produced £8,500. The whole of this land was purchased within these 20 years for £512." This was followed by the further sale of a cloth factory in the Kings Road, Chelsea, to form a square there. Whether Francis and Sophie were acting together is unclear.

In April 1826 it was reported that the couple had finally separated, with one newspaper commenting that it had "never thought them very united".[12] This immediately followed a "grand fancy dress ball" for the benefit of Italian and Spanish refugees of which Sophia was a patroness. She was described as one of 14 "fashionables" at the dinner.

Gossip writers were quick to use irony in reports about her and sometimes downright rudeness. When one of her protegées, an Italian soprano, called her "a charming person, the best natured and most amiable creature breathing, to say nothing of her comeliness", Sophia was described separately as "that foolish, fat old woman".[13] A year later, the same publication called her "a charming, sparkling petite figure, inspired with a most vivacious spirit and speaking repartee with her eloquent eyes."[14]

Francis had never broken his links with Italy and eventually he headed off to set up home in Naples with his mistress, Madame Visconti of Milan. Greville described her as "once a magnificent beauty" who "though no longer young, had fine remains of good looks and was eminently pleasing and attractive". Sophia was undaunted, continuing to provide her absent husband with an agreed allowance regardless of his absence.

**The music plays on**

The musical entertainments at Wimbledon continued too. Baron von Neumann may or may not have improved his knowledge of music but he certainly became a tough critic. At a dinner with Sophia and other friends on 8th April 1828, he heard a performance by a renowned opera singer of the day, Mademoiselle Henrietta Sontag. He commented afterwards: "Her voice which is wonderfully flexible, skims over the greatest difficulties rather than overcomes them." The singer must have enjoyed herself as she was back the following year, staying at Warren House.

At the end of September 1828 the Baron met Sophia again at a shooting party at Lord Hertford's Sudbourn home and on 22nd December she invited him to attend a performance of Rossini's opera "L'Inganno Felice" by artists from the Academy of Music. He afterwards dismissed all but two of the performers as "very ordinary".

While the music played, Sophia's money continued to flow. The year 1829 began with her presence as a guest at Mrs Fitzherbert's grand fancy ball in Brighton and she later joined the King's birthday celebrations. A magazine commentator referred to "...smiling forever, like the Countess St Antonio and her new set of patent teeth."[15] Despite everything, Francis was back after three years and in October 1829, von Neumann visited them both in Wimbledon on three successive evenings.

Two months earlier following the death of Baldassarre Platamone, Francis had officially become the Duke of Cannizzaro on the authority of the King of the Two Sicilies. His elder son Michele was now Prince Ladaria. Whether money was exchanged to bring this about is unclear as Michele might have expected to become Duke of Cannizzaro himself. However, when Baron von Neumann dined with Sophia once again at Lord Hertford's home on 7th February 1830, accompanied by Princess Esterhazy and the Duke of Wellington, Sophia was clearly relishing her new title of Duchess. She would be known as such for the rest of her life. The name Cannizzaro (albeit with different spelling) would henceforth be linked with Wimbledon forever, outliving both Sophia and Francis by well over 150 years.

Being a Duchess did Sophia no harm at all. Just a week later she was among the Duke of Wellington's guests at his home, Apsley House, London's most prestigious private address. At the same time her name continued to feature in other people's scandals as well as her own. In March 1830 the House of Lords discussed Lord Ellenborough's divorce bill against his wife after she had been seen cavorting with her lover, Prince Schwartzenberg, in his carriage, yards from Sophia's front door in Wimbledon. Lady Ellenborough had just been dining with the Duchess of Cannizaro.[16]

Sophia's musical entertainments also continued to attract big names to Wimbledon. On 15th April 1830, the famous actress Fanny Kemble appeared at her house, described by von Neumann who was also present as "not looking so pretty as she does on stage".

King George IV died on 26th June 1830 and the Duke of Cannizzaro's relationship with his Milanese mistress apparently waxed and waned. But this did not stop his return to Italy where his affairs attracted public attention alongside the great political issues of the day. In a letter from Rome dated

24th December 1830, Lord Hertford wrote to the British diplomat Thomas Raikes in St Petersburg that in Milan he had found "the Duke of Cannizzaro in great force though deserted by his Visconti for a younger man".[17]

Francis moved to Naples but in February 1832 he was back, seeking an increase to his allowance. Sophia would not agree to it. *The Morning Chronicle* reported: "The macaroni Duke of Cannizzaro has found his way back to England from his lodgings in Naples. The Duchess receives her dividends in a few days." Whether or not this embarrassed Francis, it did not stop his meeting King William IV at St James's Palace.

At the end of the year, *The Satirist* wrote mockingly: "The Duchess of Cannizzaro is here, bearing her Neapolitan honours if nothing else full well upon her. The Duke - he of scent and frippery, and foreign paste and patchwork - is not her companion and the widowed wife, and glory be unto her, shines through the mist of fashion like a lonely sherry bottle through a cloud of sawdust in the cellar of her late father. The Duke we hear is at Naples but is expected over when his lady's dividends fall due."

The music played on. In 1833, Sophia engaged two of the greatest opera singers of the day, Pasta and Malibran, to perform the duet from Rossini's "Semiramide". On another occasion that year she hosted a concert attended both by the Duke of Wellington and Lucien Bonaparte, younger brother of the late French Emperor, Napoleon. This may have been the occasion when she received a gift from Lucien of two girandoles (possibly ear-rings or pendants), said to be "of splendid workmanship and estimated to have cost 800 pounds sterling", a prodigious sum, according to a catalogue dated many years later.[18]

Some 18 years after the Battle of Waterloo, the name Bonaparte still aroused strong emotions. If Lucien thought his gift to the Duchess of Cannizzaro would assist his standing in the highest echelons of English society 12 years after his exiled brother's death in St Helena, he may have been disappointed.

The Duchess of Dino, also at the event, says in her diary: "I saw him beg [the Duchess of Cannizzaro] to introduce him to the Duke of Wellington who was present. She added: "I saw him cross the room and come up bowing and scraping to be presented to the victor of Waterloo whose reception was as cold as such baseness deserved."[19]

In August that year a newspaper reported: "The Duchess of Cannizzaro, after a season of unexampled fatigue, has taken up her rest for the autumn at Wimbledon. Her Grace has during the season, by her affability and

*Sophia Johnstone, Duchess of Cannizzaro*

kindness added many recruits to her already numerous train of admirers."[20]
But however popular she was, Sophia had no better luck in retaining her husband despite his occasional trips back to England. *The Satirist* reported on 13th July 1834 that Francis had "presented himself in affected penitential submission to the Duchess, his wife, who received him most cordially and placed largely at his disposal that which he stood greatly in need of, money. While the fat and fair Duchess was indulging in the dream that she had reclaimed the wild and roving disposition of her libertine husband, he having made free use of her coffers, suddenly decamped to the continent."
Greville details what happened next. "When she found that he had gone off without notice or warning, she first fell into violent fits of grief, which were rather ludicrous than affecting, and then set off in pursuit of her faithless lord. She got to Dover where the sight of the rolling billows terrified her so much that after three days of doubt whether she would cross the water or not she resolved to return and weep away her vexation in London.
"Not long afterwards, however, she plucked up courage and taking advantage of a smooth sea she ventured over the Straits and set off for Milan, if not to recover her fugitive better half, at all events to terrify her rival and disturb

their joys. The advent of the Cannizzaro woman was to the Visconti like the irruption of the Huns of old.

"She fled to a villa near Milan which she proceeded to garrison and fortify but finding that the other was not provided with any implements for a siege and did not stir from Milan, she ventured to return to the city and for some time these ancient heroines drove about the town glaring defiance and hate at each other, which was the whole amount of the hostilities that took place between them.

"Finding her husband was irrecoverable she at length got tired of the hopeless pursuit and resolved to return home and console herself with her music and whatever other gratifications she could command."

The relationship now seems to have passed the point of no return. In June 1835 the Duke was among several titled people prosecuted and fined by magistrates at Queen Square for not displaying his full name on his carriage, then a legal requirement for tax purposes.[21] It is unclear who paid the fine or even if he was in London at the time but he was clearly avoiding Sophia now. He was reported to have left Paris promptly in the same year on hearing that she would be hosting a musical event there.

However, Sophia found some emotional solace. Attached to a series of Italian musicians over the years she had even tried her hand at composing an overture for one of them. Soon after her confrontation with Madame Visconti she fell for a "fiddler at a second-rate theatre in Milan" and took him home to England to live openly with her, according to Greville. For the Italian this turned out to be "the most profitable business he could engage in".

The man's name was Cartagenova and she engaged him as her personal singer for the vast sum of £6000, a figure he later demanded be raised to £10,000.[22] "Di Novo", as he was called in the gossip columns, created a stir in society with Sophia described as the "fat, fair and fifty vixen" who was demanding his constant attention and giving him "the wages of prostitution".[23]

Greville wrote: "There was not the slightest attempt to conceal their connexion; on the contrary it was most ostentatiously exhibited to the world but the world agreed to treat it as a joke and do nothing but laugh at it. The only difference the 'Duchesse' ever found was that her Sunday parties [in Wimbledon] were less well attended but this was because the world (which often grows religious but never grows moral) had begun to take it into its head that it would keep holy the Sabbath night."

Surprisingly, the Chit-Chat column of *The Satirist* reported in July 1836:

"The Duchess of Cannizzaro at the close of the present season accompanied by her 'trusty and well-beloved' Di Novo...proceeds to Naples on a short visit to her Grace's husband." One can only speculate on the trip's success but the gossip became ever more vicious as time passed.

At the same time, Sophia's society status seems to have been untouched by the scandal. In its coverage of "fashionable intelligence" that September, the journal *John Bull*'s report of the busy lives of royalty also included: "The Duchess of Cannizzaro continues at her beautiful villa at Wimbledon, enjoying the society of a few select friends." At Christmas she was even welcoming Di Novo's father and sister on a visit from Italy, while visitors to her Wimbledon home a few months later included the Duke of Wellington and Marquess of Hertford.

As Queen Victoria succeeded to the throne in 1837, Sophia's entire world revolved around music, society and the substitute for her husband. In October that year *John Bull* reported: "The Duchess of Cannizzaro who passes most of her time at her delightful villa on Wimbledon Common, gives frequent musical soirees to the resident neighbouring nobility and some celebrated amateurs from town."

But despite her very real patronage of cultural life, the contrast between Sophia and the virtuous young monarch was a constant gift to gossip writers. One wrote: "The Duchess and her creature Di Novo are the only people allowed to use the royal entrance at the opera. That a male prostitute and a woman of blighted reputation should pollute the path of our maiden Queen is a little out of character but that the pair should wish to avoid observation and the blasting breath of virtuous indignation is not at all to be wondered at." [24]

Even this was mild compared with the outrageous piece that appeared on 22nd July 1838. This said: "The indecency of the woman is much upon a par with the mercenary and degraded condition of the man. We are aware that Cannizzaro received the hireling reptile in a chair which she has had so constructed as to accommodate itself to her immense size. If we were to detail one half we know in regard to this shameless pair it would be impossible - ceremoniously immoral as are those moving in the higher circles - to admit the woman into society again. As regards the reptile Di Novo, it is impossible for language to do justice to the baseness of the man who in the degraded condition in which he lives, approaches nearer to the beast than the human being. It is only surprising to us that men and women can be found so lost to every sense of feeling or decency as to admit the one or the other into their presence. In the middle and lower classes of life, parties charged with such monstrous depravity would be thrust forever out of society."

The Duke, exiled on the continent, had no further contribution to make as Sophia's last three years passed in a constant run of dinners, concerts, parties and public appearances, accompanied by endless comment. Among these was her presentation to the young Queen at a grand fete organised by the Duke of Somerset in Wimbledon Park in July 1839.

By 1838, Baron von Neumann's diplomatic career had taken him to Italy and on 28$^{th}$ August he visited the Duke of Cannizzaro's little villa at Santa Croce by the Italian lakes. The villa was "a very charming place", he wrote, although he was only able to see the downstairs rooms, occupied then by a Lady Clare. A month later in Genoa he met the Duke, "one of my old friends whom I found quite unchanged".

Sophia died on 3$^{rd}$ January 1841 having refused an operation for a hernia until it was too late and "after an illness lasting only 36 hours", according to von Neumann. As she lay dying, she sent for Di Novo who came to her bedside for a last solemn but affectionate talk. Immediately after she expired, her solicitor suggested he leave the house which he did and never set foot there again. In the five years since his arrival, he had received £20,000 for his services.[25]

Sophia had bequeathed her remaining fortune of some £40,000 entirely to the Duke in the words of Greville "notwithstanding his infidelities and his absence". Nevertheless, Francis, then living in Florence, made no attempt to attend her funeral at St Marylebone Church. The event was strictly private as she had requested in her will, attended by just a few friends and none of those whose careers she had patronised over the years.

Greville reported Sophia's death in his diary ten days after the event: "The other day died the Duchess of Cannizzaro, a woman of rather amusing notoriety whom the world laughed with and laughed at while she was alive and will regret a little because she contributed to their entertainment."

*John Bull* had earlier said: "There never lived a kinder hearted person. Her main object appeared to be the happiness of those with whom she associated. Her devotion to music and her liberal encouragement of the profession of the art were remarkable."

More tellingly perhaps *The Era* reported: "All foreigners, singers of talent, found a liberal patroness in the Duchess but we are sorry to say that her patronage and liberality was in too many instances returned with the blackest ingratitude. The ensuing season will make many of these feel the loss they have sustained in the hospitality, kindness and in many instances pecuniary support, which was extended to them by the late Duchess."

**The Duke Returns**

On 10th April 1841, Baron von Neumann was dining with Sophia's family when they were joined by the Duke who had come from Palermo to take possession of his late wife's property. He promptly ordered the sale of the entire contents of their former Wimbledon home, including the music library, books and prints. On 9th June 1841, Christie's auctioned 83 Greek vases, six marbles and a tapestry. A census taker found the mansion empty, in the care of servants. The Duke had returned to Italy for the last time.
On 23rd October, von Neumann returned from two nights at Kew with the Duke and Duchess of Cambridge to hear that the Duke of Cannizzaro too had died in Como. According to Thomas Raikes he had been "poisoned by overdoing the homeopathic system". However *The Times* attributed his demise to "taking three pills at a time which his physicians had ordered him to take only at intervals of eight hours".
It is hard to say how upset von Neumann was by the news. His diary entry simply continues by describing a trip the same evening to Haymarket to see a play by Bulwer-Lytton, "The Lady of Lyons". He thought it "a feeble piece, the principal part being badly played" while two follow-up pieces were "indifferently rendered, the actresses being common and vulgar". Of the Duke of Cannizzaro he wrote not another word.
Despite his unreasonable treatment of Sophia, Francis did not forget her family on his own death. Where she had simply left all of her property to him, he bequeathed £1000 each to her spinster nieces Emily and Sophia Augusta. The sisters were then living in Chapel Street, Grosvenor, Square. He left the same amount to their brother George Bueller, adding a colour portrait of Queen Victoria to the legacy.
The Duke's will mentions a man named Smith, an old servant of the Duchess who had worked for her for many years and still lived at Hanover Square. He was left £200. Apart from £400 left to a friend in France and unspecified amounts for his own brother and sister, the Duke of Cannizzaro left everything else to be handled by his solicitor, Francis Broderick, who also received £1000 in his own right.

The *London Gazette* 3rd December 1841 said: "All persons having any claims or demands against the English estate of the late Duke of Cannizzaro who formerly resided in Hanover Square, London, are requested to send the particulars to Messrs Powell & Co, No 9 New Square, Lincolns Inn, London."

The Wimbledon census taker was unsure how to spell the title when he visited the empty home in June 1841.[26] The former Warren House was now recorded as "Cannazerro House". In the Ordnance Survey of 1865 it appeared as "Cennezero House". Not until 1874 did the Post Office Directory register it as "Cannizaro House". So it remains.

*Cdre George Johnstone*
*(National Galleries of Scotland)*

# NOTES

1. *Oblate Communications,* 2003
2. Signed 11th June 1841. National Archives
3. *Greville Memoirs,* 1837-52 Part 2, 1885
4. *Memoirs of the Duchess of Dino,* William Heinemann, 1909
5. Collection of Wimbledon Museum of Local History
6. *Cannizaro House and its Park,* W Myson and JG Berry, 1972
7. *Town and Country Magazine,* 13th October 1781
8. *Bombast and Broadside, The Lives of George Johnstone,* R Fabel, 1987
9. *Cannizaro and its Duchess,* Francis Colmer, 1949 (Manuscript in Wimbledon Museum)
10: *Diary of Philip von Neumann 1819-33,* Philip Allan & Co Ltd, 1928
11. *The Times,* 7th October 1824
12. *The Age,* 13th April 1826
13. *The Age,* 15th April 1827
14. *The Age,* 13th April 1828
15. *Monthly Magazine,* May 1829
16. *The Times,* 10th March 1830
17. Private correspondence of Thomas Raikes with the Duke of Wellington, Richard Bentley, 1861
18. Madame Toussaud and Sons catalogue, 1866
19. *Memoirs of the Duchess of Dino,* William Heinemann, 1909. (Lucien Bonaparte was unpopular. Elsewhere she refers contemptuously to a "rather abject letter" in which he begged the Duke of Orleans to get him the job of French Minister at Florence.)
20. *The Satirist,* 18th August 1833
21. *Bells Life in London,* 15th June 1835
22. *The Satirist,* 3rd April 1836
23. *The Satirist,* 18th September 1836
24. *The Satirist,* 24th December 1837
25. *The Satirist,* 31st January 1841
26: *Cannizaro House and its Park,* R Milward, 1991

# Chapter 3: Three centuries

The full story of Cannizaro Park dates back to the early 1570s when Sir Thomas Cecil, later Lord of the Manor, created a deer hunting area of nearly 300 acres west of Wimbledon Common. In time it became known as the Old Park to distinguish it from the New Park across the Common which later became Wimbledon Park. That was designed by Lancelot Capability Brown for another Lord of the Manor, Earl Spencer in the 18$^{th}$ century.

Brown never turned his attention to the Old Park and it was a namesake who first established an identity there. In 1705, William Browne, a London merchant, bought what had by then become a successful rabbit breeding centre known as The Warren. In 1710 he built two large houses on the estate, Warren House and Westside House, living with his mistress Anne Needham in the latter while leasing what would later become Cannizaro House to friends.

The small community of Wimbledon centred on St Mary's Church in the village. Browne made a mark by clashing with the vicar, Edward Collins, over the raising of fees for baptisms, marriages and burials. In 1722 he disrupted a Sunday service by storming out of his pew as the vicar entered his pulpit and slamming the church door behind him. He repeated this performance on at least eight Sundays and at a meeting of the Vestry he called the vicar a "rogue, robber of the church and cozener of the poor".[1]

It made him enemies. The churchwardens sided with Rev Collins and denounced Browne to the Archbishop of Canterbury. In 1724 the Warren estate owner was found guilty of defamation, ordered to pay the vicar £20 in compensation, and eventually excommunicated. He died in 1738 and although both he and Anne were later buried in St Mary's churchyard, the word "dung" was irreverently added to his name in the burial register.

The estate was purchased for £6000 by a wealthy landowner, Thomas Walker (1664-1748) who had become Surveyor General of the Land Revenue in 1731 and an MP in 1733 at the advanced age of 69. He was to represent three different constituencies in Cornwall, two of them while living in Wimbledon.

His main home was in Clifford Street, off Bond Street, where he amassed a fine collection of paintings including a Van Dyck now in the National Portrait Gallery.

Interestingly, Walker himself appears in a work, possibly by Hogarth, in which he is being shown a painting. This was given to the letter writer Horace Walpole, son of Britain's first Prime Minister, Sir Robert Walpole, of whom Walker was apparently an intimate friend.[2] Horace hung it in his villa at Strawberry Hill but he doesn't appear to have thought much of Walker, describing him as "a kind of toad-eater to Sir Robert Walpole and Lord Godolphin, a great frequenter of Newmarket, and a notorious usurer".

Like Browne before him, Walker is believed to have lived in Westside House and leased Warren House to friends. He tried to make amends for Browne's earlier behaviour by acting as a churchwarden and lending the Vestry officials £50 interest-free. It was small beer. He died in October 1748 leaving an estimated £300,000 - a vast fortune then. The estate passed to his nephew, Stephen Skynner, and then to Skynner's daughter Deborah. She married Thomas Grosvenor of Swell, Somerset, and from 1769-1827 the Grosvenor family leased it to wealthy tenants. With the Count and Countess St Antonio then in residence, it passed in turn to the Drax family of Dorset in 1827 and continued to provide income to absentee landlords for the century that followed.

Thomas Walker's parkland estate appears on a map from 1746 published by the cartographer John Rocque.[3] This shows the pleasure grounds including gardens and plantations along with the fish pond and Kitchen Garden surrounded by the same high wall we see today around the Italian Garden. Beyond lay a copse with large open fields for grazing cattle, now the Royal Wimbledon Golf Course. The estate leased after 1748 covered some 60 acres with shooting rights over 130 acres of Warren Farm beyond.

## Leaseholders in the 18th century

The first notable leaseholder was yet another namesake of the founder, this time Lyde Browne, a director of the Bank of England, who lived there from 1757-85, inheriting Walker's specially created pew in St Mary's. Ten years before his arrival in Wimbledon he had begun collecting classical antiques and had become a member of the Society of Antiquaries of London in 1752.[4] For the rest of his life he accumulated a huge collection of classical (mainly

Italian) sculptures and other artworks including paintings and gems, displaying them at Warren House and establishing a link between the estate and the arts that continues right to the present day. Catalogues of the collection compiled in 1768 and 1779 showed that most of the pieces were obtained from private galleries in Rome but he bought pieces from elsewhere too.

In 1784 he negotiated a substantial sale to Empress Catherine the Great of Russia for £23,000 and it left Wimbledon in 1785. Part of it can still be seen today in the State Hermitage Museum, St Petersburg (including a rare sculpture by Michelangelo Buonarroti) as well as at Pavlovsk Palace, built by Catherine for her son and successor, Tsar Paul. However, good fortune had run out for Lyde Browne. His St Petersburg agent only paid him £10,000 of the £23,000 before going bust and the shock brought on a stroke which killed him in 1787. Another 80 collection items were sold the following year.

The Warren House lease had passed in 1785 to the Scottish lawyer and politician Henry Dundas (1742-1811), then Treasurer of the Navy. He was also a powerful member of the Board of Control for India who conflicted with George Johnstone, father of the later Duchess of Cannizzaro, over treatment of Indians. At the time it was the end of the road for Johnstone but Dundas was heading for greater things.

He was Home Secretary from 1791 under Prime Minister William Pitt the Younger and then Secretary of State for War from 1794-1801. Elevated to the peerage as Viscount Melville in 1802, he lived at Warren House until 1806, also leasing Westside House from 1791 for his family. His son Robert, second Viscount Melville, renewed that lease in 1820, remaining until 1822.

Dundas had no partner in his early years at Warren House, having divorced her first wife, the heiress Elizabeth Rennie, after she eloped with an army officer. His 1791 marriage proposal to a neighbour and fellow Scot, Lady Anne Lindsay of Gothic Lodge, Woodhayes Road, was rejected and she married Alfred Barnard, son of the Bishop of Limerick, instead. However, two years later Dundas did marry Lady Jane Hope, daughter of one of Scotland's wealthiest figures but 20 years his junior.[5] He planted beech trees in what became known as Lady Jane's Wood to celebrate their wedding. The wood remains to this day and some original beeches survived right into the 1990s. Different strands of Dundas's life tended to overlap.[6] He was instrumental in organising Britain's annexation of the Cape of Good Hope but he also arranged for Alfred Barnard to become Colonial Secretary there. Then, Lady Anne sent Lady Jane some South African bulbs for planting in the garden at Warren House. It was another example of the couple's landscaping involvement with what would later become Cannizaro Park, although where the bulbs were actually planted is unknown.

*The first Viscount Melville*

It was Lady Jane who insisted that a room be set aside for Prime Minister Pitt during his frequent visits to Warren House. However, the marriage itself was not happy and she was described as "unsuitable" for Dundas. He and the late George Johnstone had this in common too, both marrying for money, status and youth rather than love.

Lady Jane may not have been entirely taken with the long drinking sessions Dundas organised for his Cabinet colleagues at the house. His wine cellar became renowned and he would carouse for hours with Pitt, Lord Grenville and others while discussing the great affairs of the nation. King George III also breakfasted there on several occasions after military reviews on Wimbledon Common.

On 27th June 1799 the *Whitehall Evening Post* reported: "Yesterday morning the King reviewed on Wimbledon Common the London and Westminster Light Horse Volunteers...The King was accompanied by their Royal Highnesses the Dukes of York, Kent, Cumberland and Gloucester...The Royal Family at the conclusion went to Mr Dundas's house where they were entertained with an elegant collation ...the King and Princes were dressed in regimentals... His Majesty rode a beautiful bay horse. He appeared among his subjects with his usual affability and gracious condescension. Mr Dundas stood by his side for most of the time."

On another occasion in 1801 the King raised a toast to Dundas in honour of a successful naval intervention in Egypt that had worked despite the King's earlier opposition.

However, Dundas fell foul of a former neighbour, the great reformer William Wilberforce, over the proposed abolition of the slave trade, even though both of them were friends of Pitt. Wilberforce had lived at the nearby Lauriston House before moving to Clapham in 1786.

Ultimately Dundas enjoyed mixed fortunes and his sparkling career ended in corruption charges. He became First Lord of the Admiralty in 1804 but aroused suspicion about his earlier financial management when acting as Treasurer of the Navy from 1782 until 1800 alongside his other posts. A commission of enquiry was appointed, reported in 1805, and brought his impeachment in 1806 before the House of Lords. It was the last of its type ever held by the upper house. Although Dundas was actually acquitted, mud had stuck and he never again held office. Financial pressures forced him to downsize to a smaller house nearby before he left Wimbledon to return to Scotland.

He died in 1811. Nevertheless his role in the history of Wimbledon was significant enough to warrant a blue commemorative plaque on Cannizaro House some two centuries after he first arrived there. Installed in the 1950s beside the Sunken Garden by what was then the John Evelyn Society, it was designed by the Wimbledon School of Art. It survived until the 21st century but then disappeared during a hotel refurbishment.

Another mutual friend of Pitt and Dundas was the young Earl of Aberdeen who replaced the latter as lease-holder of Warren House. Many years later in 1852 he would become Prime Minister but that was long after he had left Wimbledon. Three further tenancies followed before the arrival of the future Duke and Duchess of Cannizzaro in 1817 and the estate's permanent change of identity.

## Victorian leaseholders

Cannizaro's impressive credentials continued after the deaths of the Duke and Duchess in 1841. The following year the lease passed to a senior Treasury official, Arthur Eden, nephew of Lord Auckland. Very briefly in 1854 the young Maharajah Duleep Singh took over the lease. He had recently been deposed as ruler of the Punjab by the East India Company and was brought to England. Cannizaro provided his introduction to English village life and he visited both local almshouses and St Mary's Church before moving on to larger premises, first in nearby Roehampton and later much further away in Norfolk.

In 1860 Cannizaro House passed to Ceylon tea plantation owner John Boustead whose family became stalwarts of the Wimbledon community. In 1879 the lease was taken over by Mrs Mary Schuster, whose late husband Leo had been chairman of the London and Brighton Railway and director of the Union Bank. She extended Cannizaro House with many additional rooms and the estate became known for its fashionable garden parties for as many as 1000 guests.

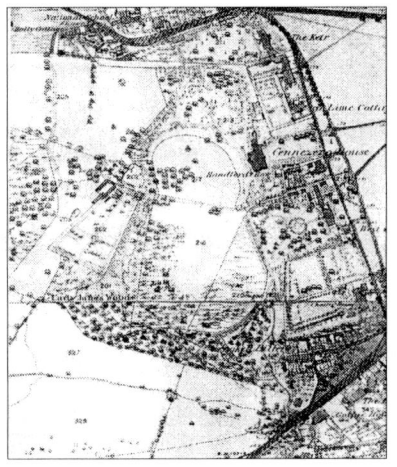

*Ordnance Survey of Cannizaro, West Side, 1865*

Mrs Schuster, formerly governess to Leo's daughter Adela, was said to be notorious for making "malaprop remarks".[7] Despite this, her visitors included the Prince and Princess of Wales and other royals including those from Spain and Denmark. She also hosted famous literary guests, including Lord Tennyson, Henry James, Max Beerbohm, and Oscar Wilde, who described the young Adela Schuster as "The Lady of Wimbledon" in his correspondence.

The ill-fated genius had good reason to admire her. She gave him £1000 for his personal use while he was on bail and he described her as "a soul that renders the common air sweet" when he was freed from Reading Prison in 1897.[8]

Like the Duchess before her, Mrs Schuster foreshadowed Cannizaro's later open air festivals with extensive musical entertainments, now held to raise funds for charity. Concerts and performances of pastoral plays were held in the grounds, among them "Fair Rosamund" based on a poem by Tennyson.[9] This was performed in 1886, using a woodland glade as a stage with the auditorium sloping gradually upwards until mingling with the trees. Tickets cost a guinea and the distinguished audience of royal and aristocratic celebrities reached their places by a side gate opening on to Caesar's Camp. In the interval they were served that now traditional fare of Wimbledon tennis fortnight, strawberries and cream. Other performances in the grounds included "Love's Labours Lost" under the patronage of several royal duchesses.[10]

The social distinctions of the day may have been immutable but poorer people were also entertained at Mrs Schuster's Cannizaro. Costermongers, girls' friendly societies and mothers' meetings were hosted there and in September 1891 an outing to Cannizaro was organised for pupils of the Ragged School, among society's poorest.[11]

After her stepmother died in 1896, Adela left Cannizaro and in 1898 bought the nearby Cottenham House in Copse Hill, a handsome villa named after Lord Chancellor the Earl of Cottenham. (Many years later she would conflict with her neighbour there, Atkinson Morley's Hospital, over marauding rabbits on her land.)

The Schusters' successor at Cannizaro was Colonel Thomas Mitchell of HM Auxiliary Forces, a renowned athlete and local magistrate, who also opened the grounds to paying visitors for good causes. In July 1899 the *Surrey Independent* reported performances of Shakespeare plays in the woods in aid of the Wimbledon Parochial Schools. There was musical accompaniment with a quartet, solo singer, an orchestra that was concealed in the woods, and "electric illuminations adding greatly to the brightness of the scene".

On another occasion Colonel and Mrs Mitchell welcomed Prince and Princess Edward of Saxe-Weimar to the formal opening of a three-day bazaar and pastoral fete. The Colonel chaired a committee to raise funds towards payment of a £5000 public debt incurred in building local primary schools for Wimbledon's rapidly growing child population. He was also involved in various good causes, including the establishment and subsequent management of the Nelson Hospital and foundation of regimental homes for soldiers.

*Pollarding work in the grounds of Cannizaro during the 1880s*

Colonel Mitchell was also the tenant of Cannizaro House when it was extensively destroyed by fire on 14th October 1900. He himself was away at the time and the house was occupied by only two of the four female servants left in charge of the building along with the lady housekeeper and the butler, neither of whom were on the premises. The fire is believed to have started in the kitchen-maid's bedroom on the top floor.[12] The flames were spotted by a passer-by across the Common in the High Street and although the local brigade rushed to the scene, firemen were seriously hampered in extinguishing the blaze quickly by an inadequate water supply, according to the official record. [13]

The damage to the building was catastrophic, although furniture, statuary, a grand piano, billiard table, pictures, books and other valuables from downstairs were rescued and transported to safety in several large pantechnicon vans. The *Surrey Independent* and *Mid-Surrey Standard* reported on 20th October: "The centre and the rear of the building - which faces the roadway - suffered most and practically the whole of the interior of that part is demolished. The two drawing, dining and other rooms on the ground floor overlooking the front lawn escaped with little damage while the servants' hall and kitchen were comparatively untouched. Happily there was little wind, else the fate of the laundry and wooden outbuildings must have been sealed while the cottages in Hanford Row would have been placed in dire peril."

The house-maid and kitchen-maid were both in shock. Had the house-maid not been bodily carried out of the building, the paper said, "she would have made her way upstairs into Mrs Mitchell's bedroom with a view to saving some of the valuables ".

The report continued: "The fire was witnessed by thousands of people, including several residents of the other large houses in the vicinity, but as only a very limited number were allowed into the grounds, the firemen were in no way inconvenienced or interrupted in their work. During the whole of the week a stream of visitors have strained their necks over the Common side of the fence to see what damage has been done but the outside appearance gives little evidence of the mischief, the walls and chimneys remaining intact throughout." Be that as it may, the delay caused by inadequate water supply led to a writ being issued by Wimbledon Council against the Southwark and Vauxhall Water Company for £114 7s 7d "for work and labour done and materials supplied".

In accordance with his lease, signed 19th May 1897, the house and estate had been insured for £9500.[14] It cost £6700 to rebuild and the Colonel was obliged to pay for some improvements himself when a new 21-year lease was agreed a year later including £750 ground rent per annum. The rebuilt property boasted electric lighting, telephones (including speaking tubes to the butler's pantry from the principal rooms), an electric burglar alarm, an improved staircase, new polished oak flooring to form a dance floor, and a verandah overlooking the lawns, a predecessor of today's hotel terrace.

An inventory in March 1900 of the entire Cannizaro estate for insurance purposes valued it at £11,875. As well as the house - whose fixtures and fittings also included a conservatory, trellises and a wooden dog kennel with iron fences - the policy covered stables for 11 horses, a coachman's dwelling, sheds, a summerhouse, gardener's cottage, vinery, five greenhouses, piggeries, bothy, and a range of other farm buildings and gates with gatekeeper's lodge.[15] Some buildings were heated by a low pressure hot water apparatus.

In the event, the Mitchells only stayed until 1904 and the lease was then taken over by a writer, linguist and convert to Buddhism, John Savile, Earl of Mexborough, who remained until his death in 1916. The house was then used as a convalescent home for army officers during the First World War. It was known as American Red Cross Hospital No 102 and those staying there enjoyed luxurious conditions far from the Western Front.

*US Army officers convalescing at Cannizaro during the First World War*

When the war was over, Cannizaro House switched back to its final leaseholder. This was Percy Chubb, safe manufacturer and a Fellow of the London Zoological Society, who lived there from 1918-19. On 11th November 1919, *The Times* reported the sale of the house's contents, left there since the death of Lord Mexborough. They fetched high prices throughout. These included 226 guineas for a satinwood bedroom suite, £490 for a salon suite, 90 guineas for an Aubusson carpet, 165 guineas for a boule commode, 60 guineas for a boule writing table, 50 guineas for a pair of Chippendale mirrors, and 85 guineas for a mirror by Kent. To set this in context, servants' wages would have been in shillings rather than pounds at the time. (There were 20 shillings to one pound and a guinea was worth one pound and one shilling).

**Final absentee landlord**

The freehold of the Cannizaro estate had been held by the Drax family since 1827 and the Grosvenors before that since 1769.[16] By the early 20th century the owner was the Hon Sir Reginald Aylmer Ranfurly Plunkett-Ernle-Erle-Drax, KCB, DSO, JP, DL (1880–1967) whose many titles, names and post-nominals marked him out and throw light on the origins of a number of

Wimbledon's local street names today.

Reginald and his elder brother, the writer Lord Dunsany, were sons of the 17th Baron of Dunsany (1853-1899) and Elizabeth Louisa Maria Grosvenor Ernle-Erle-Drax (1855-1916), née Burton. It has been suggested that the family may have inspired some of the fanciful aristocrats created by writers such as PG Wodehouse and Evelyn Waugh.

In fact Sir Reginald Drax became a Royal Navy captain after serving in the Battle of Jutland in 1916 and nearly changed the face of history at the start of the Second World War. Enjoying a notable diplomatic career, in August 1939 he led a failed attempt to form an Anglo-French alliance with the Soviet Union. Had he succeeded he might have pre-empted the Molotov-Ribbentrop pact which gave Hitler free range over eastern Europe before attacking Russia two years later. Despite the failure, Drax was later heavily involved with the Atlantic convoys that kept Britain going during the war's darkest days.

He had an instinct for the dramatic. Years before, while director of the Naval Staff College at Greenwich, he had set the ball rolling for the eventual transformation of his property in Wimbledon by starting to sell off all the land and buildings of the original Old Park for potential development.

Westside House was leased once more to an American heiress who turned it into a Theosophist Centre. But the departure of Percy Chubb from Cannizaro House was followed by sale of the freehold itself in February 1920 for £30,750 to Edward Kenneth Wilson, director of the Ellerman and Wilson shipping line and a Lloyds underwriter. He had first expressed interest in the property back in 1914.

It was only after intervention by the John Evelyn Society that the borough council stopped further development on the Royal Wimbledon Golf Course, leased by the club since 1907. In 1938, rather than see the course disappear, Wimbledon Council paid Drax £151,000 for the freehold on 140 acres, leasing it back to the club for 50 years. It has since been extended virtually in perpetuity.

Drax sold the last remaining eight acres of Warren Farm to Leslie Hore-Belisha, who introduced the Belisha beacon when Minister of Transport. He was also War Minister from 1937-40 under Neville Chamberlain. Hore-Belisha sold off the last cattle that grazed there, ending its livestock breeding role after some three centuries. Warren Farm has been in private hands ever since, separated from Cannizaro by the golf course and now associated with the Common rather than the modern park. The Cannizaro estate was beginning to look a little more like the park we know today.

**Seeds of the modern park**

Edward Kenneth Wilson's arrival at Cannizaro marked far more than just a change of freehold ownership. Surprisingly perhaps in view of its subsequent importance, the estate's social prestige before 1920 had not been matched by a particularly imaginative approach to its horticulture or even its landscaping since the time of Henry Dundas. With Capability Brown and his namesake's attention elsewhere in the 18th century and little evidence of the 19th century leaseholders following the Victorian fashion for plant collecting, the grounds of Cannizaro generally reflected native species and natural rather than cultivated beauty.

Some leaseholders were interested in the grounds as well as the house. The Edwardian Buddhist Lord Mexborough was said to be a keen gardener and some trees were planted by others but there are few really ancient specimens today apart from those in Lady Jane's Wood and the stunted oaks on the upper lawn near the statue of Diana and the Fawn. One hollow stump is estimated at 300 years old. The biggest oak, in the Mediterranean Garden on the lower slope, is some 25 metres in height with the girth of over two metres. William Browne might just have spotted it in the early 18th century.

*The Wilsons with designer George Dillistone and head gardener William Allison*

The real change came after 1920. As members of both the Rhododendron Society and the Royal Horticultural Society, Wilson and his wife Adela (also known as Molly) can take much of the credit for the many rare trees and shrubs that justify today's English Heritage Grade II* registration. They did give credit to earlier plantings where this was due. On 26th August 1923, Wilson wrote to *The Times* on the subject of black walnut trees, claiming one at Cannizaro had been planted by Dundas.

But the change came when they employed landscape architect George Dillistone to lay out a new garden. This led to the creation of the rhododendron, camellia and magnolia walks in Lady Jane's Wood and planting of many unusual shrubs and trees from North America and the Far East. They also established both the Maple Avenue leading to the Diana statue (moved from outside the verandah to its current position) and the Sunken Garden, then a fashionable innovation.

These were major infrastructural changes to the grounds but the Wilsons were equally involved in growing award-winning specimens for competitions. On 15th January 1936, *The Times* reported Wilson's entry at the Royal Horticultural Show, an orchid entitled Cannizaro. In August the same year at another RHS show, he exhibited a variety of *Cattleya Loddigesii*. On 27th July 1938 the paper carried a letter from him reporting the amount of rainfall between 1935 and 1938 and emphasising the drought of that year. No previous occupants of Cannizaro or Warren House before it had ever been so completely dedicated to beautifying the estate or improving its natural advantages.

The Wilsons had first moved to Roehampton from an estate near Hull in Yorkshire but they now stayed at Cannizaro for the rest of their lives. The wrought iron gate at the main entrance still bears his "EKW" monogram. It was brought from Roehampton House in 1920 and moved from the bottom of the Kitchen Garden in 1948.

They also brought their head gardener, William Allison, and his family from Yorkshire. He took up the same post at Cannizaro, serving the Wilsons for 50 years until his death in August 1946. His son Richard succeeded him in the job, matching his father's record by remaining at Cannizaro long after the estate had become publicly owned. He finally retired on 6th November 1970. Richard and Ida Allison lived with their son Billy in an 18th century cottage beside the pond, staying right up to his retirement. Sadly, the cottage was demolished soon afterwards to save renovation costs.

Like their predecessors at Cannizaro, the Wilsons also had other staff living on the estate. Wimbledon Council's Buildings and Improvements Committee approved alterations and additions to the entrance lodge on 19th November 1920 and then construction of new bungalows in the grounds in January and November 1925. Keir Cottage in Camp Road was occupied by their butler, Mr Key, and his wife. They too would remain long after the estate's takeover by the local authority. Only when Mr Key died in the 1960s, would his widow move away.

Keen dog-lovers, the family had several pets and created their own dogs cemetery in the grounds. This would survive as a point of interest right into the 1990s until being fenced off, the little stones broken and neglected. Figures of dogs can still be seen on the gates of the Dutch Garden, created later on the former site of the stables and coachman's dwelling. How the Wilsons' dogs reacted to the sheep that were still grazing in the grounds in the 1920s is unrecorded.

In 1932, Wilson bought the neighbouring property, The Keir, to head off another housing development plan. Having secured the land and extended Cannizaro accordingly, he re-sold The Keir itself with a reduced area of space for continued use as its own garden.[17]

The precedents that had been set by Mrs Schuster and Colonel Mitchell in offering use of the grounds for charitable events continued under the Wilsons. On 12th July 1929 *The Times* reported that they had lent the gardens to the organisers of a fete. As in the Colonel's day, this was to raise funds for the Nelson Hospital. The grounds opened to the public again in spring 1935.

The Guides Chapel by Camp Road, one-time home of a Catholic priest, had previously belonged to The Keir. During the 1930s the Wilsons invited the local Brownies and Girl Guides to use both this building and the recently added part of the former Keir Garden for games and singing. Their daughter Hilary is believed to have belonged to the organisation and the Wilsons certainly took great interest in it. An international jamboree camp was held in the grounds of Cannizaro shortly before the Second World War.

They bequeathed the chapel to the local Brownies and a pack continued to use it as their lair until moving away to newly built accommodation in the 1950s. However, the link remains to this day. Brownie Revels have traditionally been held there bi-annually and Sunday teas are served to the public from the building each summer.

The Wilsons were more generous than their predecessors in allowing local residents access to the gardens. Adela would often chat with them and point out particular plants in bloom. During the Second World War the couple lent the land to residents for use as rent-free allotments. In order to access their produce the holders would walk down Camp Road, enter through a gate beside Diana, and walk back through the grounds along a track known as the "cinder road". There were no sheds for storage so they brought their own gardening tools each visit.

Today's allotments lie on what was formerly the 18th hole of the Royal Wimbledon Golf Course. The wartime allotments actually covered a much larger area of the estate than today, most of which was restored to parkland in 1949.

After the inspired garden designing of the 1920s and 30s, the war took its toll on the estate in a number of ways. Cannizaro was used for exercises by the Home Guard and its maintenance was neglected. The rhododendrons became overgrown and honey fungus became widespread. A bomb demolished a bungalow directly opposite what is now the site of the Aviary. Two people were killed, including a retired employee of the Wilsons. The site was cleared of rubble and a gardener, Mr Chapman, was later busily preparing the ground for Jerusalem artichokes when he unearthed the clock mechanism of an unexploded 500lb bomb. Despite the damage it had never actually exploded. Had it done so, much of Cannizaro might have gone up too.

**African icon**

A bust of the last Ethiopian Emperor, Haile Selassie, now stands in the Old Tennis Garden amid the rhododendron bushes. Previously located outside Keir Cottage, it was moved to its present position in 1985 and underwent a major restoration in 2005. The artist, Hilda Seligman, was a neighbour of the Wilsons across the common at Lincoln House on Parkside. She and her relatives campaigned on behalf of the Emperor, providing a refuge for him and his family when they were driven into exile by the Italian invasion of their country, then called Abyssinia, in 1935.

The iconic bust was given to the local authority when Lincoln House was demolished in 1957. It depicts one of the most significant historical figures now associated with Cannizaro yet there is no evidence that Haile Selassie actually visited the Wilsons during his stay in Wimbledon. The British Government of the day had tried to appease Mussolini by refusing the imperial family entry to the country but the Seligman family overcame this resistance and took him into their home.

From his base in Wimbledon, Haile Selassie made several trips to Geneva to plead his country's case to the League of Nations. He also met black groups in London including Marcus Garvey's United Negro Improvement Association and spoke at many public meetings. When it became clear that a rapid return home was not on the cards, he bought a house in Bath and moved there.

He had to wait until Britain was at war before flying to Sudan in 1940 and leading a liberation campaign to free Abyssinia with British military support. From 1941 he was back in power and donated his house in Bath as a local residence for the elderly. He returned to Wimbledon to see the Seligmans again after the Second World War and younger members of the family later visited him in Ethiopia.

When Hilda Seligman's sculpture of the Emperor was restored in 2005, it was formally unveiled by the Mayor of Merton in the presence of both exiled Ethiopian imperial and Seligman family members, as well as Rastafarian followers of Haile Selassie. It was another historic moment for Cannizaro.

*Hilda Seligman (left) and family with Haile Selassie after the war*

**The final curtain**

Adela Wilson died on 23$^{rd}$ August 1946, followed on 1$^{st}$ February 1947 by her husband. They had celebrated their golden wedding the previous year.

During their time at Cannizaro they had created such a spectacular garden that even the neglect of the war years could not hide its value as a horticultural collection and place of beauty to be treasured.

Their daughter Hilary had married the 5th Earl of Munster on 10th July 1928 at a wedding with a long list of distinguished guests as reported in *The Times*. Exactly 20 years later, she sold the entire estate to Wimbledon Council. Combined with the land of Westside House, purchased at the same time, the gardens became available for permanent public access and Cannizaro Park came into being.

Hilary's husband, Geoffrey William Richard Hugh FitzClarence (1906-75), was the great-great-grandson of King William IV and his mistress, Dorothy Jordan. He succeeded to his title in the same year as his wedding and became a prominent politician, holding ministerial office under five Prime Ministers. Also Lord Lieutenant of Surrey from 1957-73, he was succeeded in the title by a second cousin whose son became the seventh and last Earl of Munster. The title died with him in 2000.

After their wedding in 1928, the Earl and Countess of Munster lived first at No 8 Hill Street and then settled at Sandhills in Bletchingley on the North Downs. In true Cannizaro tradition, Hilary was a great lover of music. A talented pianist herself, in 1958 she founded the Countess of Munster Musical Trust to help young musicians achieve their full potential as performers. Her endowment now provides assistance to young musicians amounting to almost £200,000 a year.

Hilary spent the following 21 years until her death in November 1979 watching her Trust's steady growth. She took a keen interest in its activities, regularly attending meetings and audition days and actively following the careers of its beneficiaries, whether singers, instrumentalists or composers.

So musical entertainment has played a significant part in the Cannizaro story, whether organised by the Duchess, by Mrs Schuster, or at a distance by the Countess of Munster. Some concerts were also performed in the years after Cannizaro became a public park, organised by the Council's library department. We can only speculate on what the estate's original residents would have thought of the more recent rock, pop and jazz of the park's open air festivals. But part of Cannizaro's special quality is its appeal to the senses - sound as well as sight and smell. Music has its own magic. It is a good fit.

## NOTES

1. *Historic Wimbledon*, R Milward, 1989
2. St Mary's Churchyard, Wimbledon
3. *Exact Survey of the Cities of London, Westminster and the Country nearly ten miles round*. J Rocque, 1746
4. *American Journal of Archaeology* 88, 1984
5. *.Notes on Cannizaro and Henry Dundas, Viscount Melville*, F Colmer, 1948 (ms in Wimbledon Museum of Local History)
6. *Notes by A W Hughes Clarke on the great houses of Wimbledon*, 1948 (ms in Wimbledon Museum of Local History)
7. *Cannizaro and its Park,* R Milward, 1991
8. *De Profundis,* O Wilde, March 1897
9. *Pall Mall Gazette*, 9th July 1886
10. *The Times*, 11th July 1891
11. *Penny Illustrated Paper*, 5th September 1891
12. *Wimbledon News*, 20th October 1900
13. *Engineer's Report on Water Supply to Cannizaro, Wimbledon Common,* Wimbledon Urban District Council 1901
14. New title deed signed by freeholder Mrs Sarah Charlotte Elizabeth Egginton-Ernle-Erle-Drax of Charborough Park, Dorset, and Thomas Mitchell, Colonel of HM Auxiliary Forces and Justice of the Peace of the County of Surrey, 17 October 1901 (Wimbledon Museum of Local History)
15. Law Union & Crown Insurance Company, 25th March 1900
16. *Notes by A W Hughes Clarke on the great houses of Wimbledon*, 1948 (ms in Wimbledon Museum of Local History)
17. The Keir land he re-sold was eventually used for Stonecourt on the corner of Camp Road. It became known as "the house that Jack built" because the horse Jack brought the building materials up Wimbledon Hill. The Keir itself was turned into flats.

# Chapter 4: Going public

Following her father's death in February 1947, Hilary, Countess of Munster, offered to sell both house and garden to Wimbledon Council for £40,000. Westside House, the neighbouring property since 1710, looked available too as the last lease-holder was not resident and Drax was unlikely to take a different view. Reunited, the entire estate offered potential for housing and allotments as well as public open space.
To be clear about the garden's value, the Council obtained a report on its content from Mr W M Campbell, Curator of Kew Gardens.[1] Dated 9th May 1947, he listed copper beech, beech, black walnut, red and scarlet oak, black birch, south beech and sweet gum among species clearly labelled as well as hundreds of small flowering and ornamental trees. These included magnolia, Judas, Indian horse chestnut, *Parrotia persica, amelanchiers, Cercidiphyllum, Sorbus*, Japanese maple, *Eucryphia pinnatifolia, acers, Crataegus*, camellias, rhododendrons and azaleas.
He wrote: "The nature of the land rules out its possible use for active games such as football, cricket and hockey but consideration could be given to the layout of hard or grass tennis courts, netball pitches and possibly putting. It would be impossible to maintain the plant collections and at the same time allow of many games being played."
The Kitchen Garden covered 2½ acres and he recommended repairing its glasshouses to grow vines, peaches and figs. He continued: "The Kitchen Garden offers an ideal area for a fruit and vegetable demonstration garden both to local ratepayers and for educational purposes in the schools. The gardens as a whole would offer ideal material for nature study for schoolchildren.
"There are so many rare trees and fine specimens involved that it would be sacrilege to dispense with them... it would call for considerable skill in order to preserve the natural beauties of the garden and at the same time link these with the various amenities that might be added for the benefit of the public."
Of Cannizaro House he wrote: "Externally it is a mansion of pleasing design and in a very good state of preservation. On its walls facing west there are a

large number of rare plants which succeed better than they do at Kew." There could be no better commendation.

On 27th May 1947, Mr T Webster, borough engineer and surveyor, wrote to the regional planning officer at the Ministry of Town and Country Planning that he had discussed the estate's purchase with Mr Nicole of the Health Ministry. The Countess of Munster had made an "attractive offer" to sell Cannizaro for open spaces, playing fields, housing and other purposes. It could be purchased under Section 10 (1) of the Town and Country Planning Act 1944.

On 9th June 1947, Edwin M Neave, Wimbledon Town Clerk, wrote to the Secretary at the Ministry of Town and Country Planning reminding him that Wimbledon Council had decided to buy Cannizaro for £40,000 freehold to provide pleasure grounds, playing pitches, allotments and housing but without preparation of details. The Council had earlier bought the freehold of the Royal Wimbledon Golf Course, he added.

Cannizaro must be unique considering its proximity to London, he said. "It has been laid out and maintained very skilfully and it has horticultural features in the way of specimen trees and avenues of trees which are exceptional."

Westside House covered 11 acres and was being converted to flats. Wimbledon Town Planning Scheme no. 1 permitted single dwelling houses only with density of four to the acre. The North East Surrey Joint Planning Committee was about to receive a recommendation that this should be reduced to just two to the acre. The Countess of Munster wanted use of the estate by either Wimbledon or Surrey Councils for the £40,000.

**Difference of opinion**

He added: "This is considered to be a very low figure and an opportunity to purchase on these terms is not considered likely to arise again." Admiral Drax, who had sold land to the Council in the past, owned Westside House which was currently let to a non-resident lessee. Its sale was probable but the price of £15,000 might require compulsory purchase. He had applied to the Ministry of Health for loan permission and a formal resolution was awaited.

However, there was no consensus between the local and national governments on the best course to follow at that stage. On 21st June Mr Nightingale of the Ministry of Town and Country Planning was clearly unenthusiastic about the purchase proposal. He said Westside was already being converted to flats and both it and Cannizaro House were "neglected and not of any special merit". There was therefore little hope of need for the Council to buy them for the stated purposes under the 1944 Act.

He continued: "The need in Wimbledon is for decentralisation of overcrowded wards and redevelopment at lower densities with the deficiencies in local open space in those wards remedied." The land was not well placed, he wrote, to serve the needs of overcrowded wards in respect of open space or allotments. Partial use for housing would provide some potential but only two houses on each site could be added and this would not solve the overcrowding problem. While the Council already had Westside House for conversion there was "little probability of Cannizaro being developed in accordance with the operative scheme".

On 8th July 1947, Edwin Neave wrote again to the Ministry of Town and Country Planning, confirming that both freeholder and leaseholder of Westside House were willing to sell to the Council. The whole property of Westside House would be converted into 90 flats (two dwellings to the acre), he said.

An internal letter within the Ministry dated 5th August questioned whether £40,000 was too high a price to pay for Cannizaro and asked if a compulsory purchase order was really needed. The writer, A L Bickford ordered a District Valuer's report. The District Valuer duly reported on 22nd August that he was prepared to approve the purchase, drawing attention to the special contracting out clauses in the 1947 Act. There was no suggestion of a delay, although Wimbledon Council was then awaiting consent of both the Ministries of Planning and Health on the question of a loan.

The Council was also awaiting the District Valuer's report on Westside House. This now proposed three blocks of dwellings comprising 54 flats and 12 blocks of houses comprising 43 dwellings.

On 22nd September 1947 Mr Neave sent the District Valuer's report of 22nd August on Cannizaro to Mr Bickford. A total of 32.5 acres were to be acquired. This was freehold, subject to leases to the Royal Wimbledon Golf course of the 1.223-acre house green for 50 years from 1944 and the 1.285-acre 16th green for which the club had a purchase option for £1050 within ten years from 6th December 1944. Each lease involved ground rent of five shillings a year.

The Countess of Munster's purchase price covered the three floors of

Cannizaro House with six reception rooms and kitchen offices on the ground floor, 14 bedrooms and three bathrooms on the first floor, and eight further bathrooms on the second floor. The estate brought with it stabling, garages, a gardener's cottage, glasshouses and men's bothy, all in sound condition except one cottage which was war damaged. Included too were the Keir and Pond Cottages, whose occupants, the Keys and Allisons, had life tenancies.

Under a mutual covenant between Cannizaro and Westside dated 12th March 1920, neither could be developed without first giving a purchase option to the other. This was for a term expiring the earlier of either 1st February 2019 or "the day on which shall expire the period of 21 years from the death of the last survivor of such of the issue of her late Majesty Queen Victoria as were living on the last day of February 1920". Such were the complexities of Drax's decision to sell Wilson the freehold on one of the two houses built by Browne in 1710 while retaining the other.

The officials reached agreement and this bizarre legal requirement became redundant. The Countess's £40,000 offer was to be accepted. As it happened, compulsory purchase terms were available anyway.

On 1st October 1947 Wimbledon Council confirmed the purchases of both Cannizaro and Westside House. Cannizaro House was to provide housing for the elderly while its land provided a site reserved for tennis courts, space for pleasure grounds or playing fields, nursery accommodation and 2.3 acres of allotments. Westside House itself would provide eight flats with additional space for new dwelling accommodation in its grounds. These would also provide either more pleasure grounds or playing fields and a further 2.1 acres of allotments.

The overall purchase package also included 0.8 acres of land for allotments behind the nearby properties White House and Bardon Lodge and sites for new dwellings to replace no 5 West Side and next to no 18 Dunstall Road.

On 22nd December 1947 Mr Neave wrote again to Mr Bickford, referring to his letter to the Health Ministry requesting sanction under the Public Health Act 1875 to borrow £41,100 for Cannizaro and £16,150 for Westside, including the extra developments at the adjoining properties. The arrangement also required an Exchequer grant under Section 94 of the Town and Country Planning Act 1947.

*Gardening staff in the Kitchen Garden in the 1950s*

**Green belt option**

There was one more aspect to the story. On 27th October 1947, Mr W J Pickering, Surrey County Planning Officer, based in County Hall, Kingston, wrote to Cyril Walker, Director of Housing and Valuer at the London County Council.[2] He said he had written to Wimbledon Council asking if it would be interested in buying Cannizaro jointly under the new green belt scheme restricting further urban spread of the capital into the neighbouring counties.

At that time before the local government reforms of 1965 and the creation of today's Greater London boroughs, Cannizaro and Westside were just under a mile from the Surrey county border. As the county town, Kingston-upon-Thames and its surrounding area lay within Surrey, not London. In view of Cannizaro's special nature, a case was made for a cash contribution. The suggestion of 25% contribution was conditional on waiting for the "appointed day" for confirmation of the purchase unless the District Valuer said there would be little saving and the owners were not prepared to wait.

Did this mean today's Cannizaro Park might have been designated as green belt land rather than a municipal park? Might the distinction have had some significance for its long-term protection? Apparently not.

On 30th January 1948, Cyril Walker reported the outcome of Surrey's green belt proposal and joint funding request. Representatives of the London County Council and Wimbledon borough had jointly visited the site to inspect it. Together, Cannizaro and Westside covered 45 acres of which part would be used for housing, eight acres for allotments and a horticultural nursery, and the remaining 30 acres or so would be preserved as open space.

Mr Walker pointed out that the site formed part of over 5000 acres of open space beyond the urban borough of Wandsworth, comprising Richmond and Bushey Parks, the Old Deer Park, Wimbledon Common and Putney Heath. He wrote: "The grounds of Cannizaro House are very well laid out and are particularly attractive from the horticultural aspect with a fine collection of ornamental shrubs, flowering trees etc. They have been inspected by the Curator of Kew Gardens who strongly recommends that they should be preserved for public use."

There were points against any London County Council contribution under the Green Belt (London and Home Counties) Act of 1938. Residences on Common Westside separated the land from Wimbledon Common itself, there were further houses both north and south of the site and the Royal Wimbledon Golf Course lay on its western border.

The green belt was intended to provide a ring of land free of development 15 miles around Charing Cross. Thanks to the enthusiastic land sales by Drax and others, it was now already too late to save Cannizaro's rural identity. It simply did not fit the criteria for green belt and really just amounted to a local park. The legal criteria for saving open space did not apply anyway since the adjacent borough of Wandsworth was not deficient under existing London County Council planning with 3.9 acres per 1000 people.

Mr Walker added: "Although London residents would doubtless visit this land and derive benefit therefrom, it is felt that the scheme is likely to be of much more benefit to the residents of Wimbledon and in particular to the residents of the local housing scheme which forms part of the borough council's proposals."

The total cost of the proposed green belt area would have been £20,000 of which the London County Council would be paying up to a third or £7000. He did not recommend such a contribution. By 19th February, Surrey had acknowledged the rejection. Cannizaro's future as a municipal park, albeit a very special one, rather than green belt, was confirmed.

*Public events in the grounds soon after public ownership.*

*Above: Greatorex Theatre at Cannizaro*
*Below: Pensioners receive tobacco plants grown at the*
*Cannizaro nursery in the old Kitchen Garden*

## NOTES

1. Report for the Borough of Wimbledon, 9th May 1947, London Metropolitan Archives. LCC/CL/PK/1/127 1947-48
2. Green Belt - Surrey - Cannizaro and West Side, Wimbledon, London Metropolitan Archives. LCC/CL/PK/1/127 1947-48

# Chapter 5: Municipal revival

Henry T Hopper, LIPA, FinstBCA (Dip), lived in a cottage at Cannizaro close to the site of the wartime bomb and knew a great deal about the place. He was also Wimbledon Council's Open Spaces and Cemetery Superintendent. In June 1955, he produced notes on the "Cannizaro Mansion House and Park",[1] writing: "Cannizaro Park, although the most recent and from a horticultural standpoint, the most important open space acquisition made by the corporation, has quickly become one of the most popular gardens in suburban London."

The Cannizaro and Westside estates together had amounted to some 45 acres. In the winter of 1948-49 the wartime allotments had been vacated and in 1949 the land cleared and re-sown. On 7th February 1949 new allotments had been allocated and by 1955, with completion of public housing in the newly created Chester and Sycamore Roads and Beech Close on what had been the West Side estate, 34 acres remained as public open space.

Cannizaro House had been leased to Surrey County Council as an old people's home. Of the grounds in the Wilsons' day before the war, Mr Hopper wrote: "The whole appearance of the estate was transformed by systematic planting of various collections under the most expert advice available." The land was very undulating with pleasing slopes in a westerly direction. He added: "There is little doubt that very few gardens in this country contain such a vast wealth of botanical and rare plants in such a small acreage, nor do many gardens possess such landscape features." However, the last years of private ownership had seen a sharp decline in the level of maintenance. The rhododendrons and azaleas had become overgrown and hundreds of beech, ash and sycamore saplings had grown, suppressing the ornamental plantings.

*Opposite page: Pinks*

In many places *Rhododendron ponticum*, previously used as a rootstock for the improved varieties, had spread into a thicket. Honey fungus was taking a severe toll and among its victims were what had been the country's tallest Sassafras tree, a superb *Madrono* and a promising *Embothrium*.

**Plentiful labour**

With a well supplied labour force under the new Council ownership, the gardens thrived again as they had done in the 1930s. Work in the early and mid-1950s included clearance of saplings throughout the main area of rhododendrons and planting of new rhododendrons beside the laburnum trees running along the east side of the Kitchen Garden wall, starting behind Pond Cottage. The host of golden daffodils still seen every spring along the main back path of the Keir Garden was first planted in those years.
Construction of Chester Road required a new tree-lined perimeter for the park on that side and limes were used, backing on to the rear gardens of the new houses. Also created in 1957-8 was the water cascade in an area then known as the Poplar Walk. A specimen of *Metasequoia glyptostraboides* was brought to the Keir Garden from Kew and cuttings from this were planted in the new Water Garden, near the pond and along the back path. Richmond Park's Isabella Plantation sourced azalea and camellia cuttings for the Azalea Dell.[2]
The park's notable trees included Indian Bean *(Catalpa Bignonioides)*, Lady's Handkerchief *(Davidia), Nyassas, Amelanchier*, cherries and the ubiquitous silver birches. The Maple Avenue was now well established with its superb autumn colours. The Keir Garden was newly planted with varieties of lilies and Kurume azaleas, a wall shrub collection, and the Rose Garden. This was to be enhanced periodically.
In 1953, a Herbaceous Border was planted on the west side of the old Kitchen Garden wall. Mr Hopper wrote two years later: "Herbaceous borders are one of the most inexpensive forms of gardening both in time and money, and this long border contains a number of attractive plants which flower in rotation during the whole of the summer." In the early 1990s the Herbaceous Border remained one of Cannizaro's loveliest features. However it was cleared when overtaken by bindweed. The high level of maintenance three times a year had by then become a reason not to restore it.
The Sunken and Dutch Gardens were among the most significant improvements

following municipal control. Mr Hopper wrote: "So much of the estate was designed for late spring and autumn effect that summer was largely ignored: now, however these two gardens are planted extensively with bedding plants of all types with the one object of achieving a riot of colour over as long a period as possible. No attempt has been made to introduce any rare plants into these gardens, bedding plants and annuals are mixed to achieve colour as quickly as possible after the finish of the spring display."

This was precisely the reverse of the policy that would be introduced 50 years later and applies today. However, rarer species were not far away. Connoisseurs Corner was created on a corner of the main lawn near the Sunken Garden. This became the place for unusual shrubs and trees, among them *Illicium floridanum, Xanthoceras sorbifolia, Albizzia julibrissin rosea*, and *Maclura aurantiaca*.

From 1960, native oak trees were planted to replace the sycamore and beech seedlings that had earlier run riot. Hollies too were abundant, some as high as ten metres, and these were encouraged in order to provide a dark background and shelter for the ornamental plants. The garden planners aimed to create outstanding colour effects, focusing on plants with silver and gold foliage. They used variegated bamboo, grasses and grass-like plants, overtopped by luxuriant eucalyptus and spangled with masses of lilies and gladioli.

**Rhododendrons and azaleas**

Shrubs that had outgrown their stations were transplanted and a new approach was taken to the park's rhododendrons. Those planted since the Council's takeover of Cannizaro had been a mixture of types with hardy hybrids popular and the ubiquitous *Rhododendron ponticum* as rootstock. However they had not all thrived and the Rhododendron pink pearl was dominant. New plantings and transplantings now took place and a range of different vistas were created. A policy was adopted of providing mass effects for the general public, interplanted with smaller groups of rare varieties to attract specialists.

The Azalea Tunnel was created in 1965 out of a tangle of boughs that had grown over a steep bank. Years earlier the bank had been planted with grafted azaleas but the rootstock *Rhododendron luteum* had become dominant and the path down the bank inaccessible. The three-metre high boughs were now laced together to form a romantic archway and steps were created down the bank from second-hand granite kerbs laid on their sides in an ascending curve.

In the 1970s permanent new features introduced to the park included the Aviary. A fountain nearby welcomed visitors from the main entrance (less ostentatious than today's Millennium Fountain) and on either side of the path towards it were brightly coloured summer bedding plants, set in grass with two or three rows of edging and elaborate knots. Beyond the fountain, the new white and gilt wooden Aviary was designed in the style of a miniature Italian cathedral and populated by budgerigars, later joined by cockatiels.

At the other end of the park beyond Lady Jane's Wood, the Belvedere was created as a startling feature with eight columns topped by carved urns and a balustrade. Completed in 1981, for a few years it overlooked the short-lived Heather Garden, a glorious sloping acre and a half of colour created for late summer flowering but sadly doomed by insufficient irrigation facilities. By the late 1990s, this large area was already replaced by the Mediterranean Garden where *cistus* plants were intended to tolerate the naturally dry conditions more successfully.

Municipal control brought moves to enhance the park's wildlife too, principally around or in the pond. At one point there was a trial introduction of swans from Richmond Park. However, this was not successful as having their wings clipped simply encouraged the birds to try returning to their old habitat on foot. Not very practical. On another occasion a large pike was added to the pond with less than satisfactory results for wildlife. The fish ate all the young ducklings. But the pond was a permanent source of fascination. One duck regularly built her nest in a hole in a nearby oak tree and her offspring had to fall some 12 feet to reach the water.

**Start of decline**

From the mid-1950s until 1970, the Kitchen Garden contained substantial glasshouses and served as a nursery for municipal floral displays throughout Wimbledon as well as further afield at the Guildford Show, Chelsea Flower Show and Surrey County Hall in Kingston. Plants from Cannizaro Park were used to decorate the town hall and public hall for civic functions.

But the great days of expansion and improvement for the park under public control were not to last. In 1965, Wimbledon's merger with Mitcham and Morden to form the London Borough of Merton brought significant transfers of personnel. For some council departments such as the libraries this meant growth. But for the parks it marked the start of the decline in gardening staff numbers and funding resources that has continued ever since. Cannizaro's team of 28 was reduced to 12 when its nursery role was taken over in 1969 by the former Peacock Farm Nursery in Lower Morden Lane. The new central nursery replaced a total of five units dispersed around the borough.

In 1970 the Council resolved to redevelop the Kitchen Garden as a series of small formal gardens: a rose garden, knot garden, ornamental vegetable garden, winter garden, small maze, jardin de treillage, and cloister garth. The former nursery buildings were to be replaced by a small field study centre and local history museum in the form of a short village street demonstrating handicrafts and manufactures. None of this materialised as Merton progressively reduced the budgets and staff available for Cannizaro.

*Cannizaro Pond, unchanged since private days*

In 1976 with the Kitchen Garden no longer used as a plant nursery, it was approved for use as a bird reserve by local birdwatchers "until such time as the land is required for development as an English Garden". This was in what later became the Italian Garden. The retirement of Richard Allison as head gardener in 1970 after 52 years left the 18th century Pond Cottage empty for the first time under public ownership. It would have cost £5500 to refurbish the little building which had repeatedly featured in romantic images of the gardens and was within the Wimbledon Village Conservation Area. The John Evelyn Society (soon to be renamed the Wimbledon Society) made proposals for its future use but Merton Council ordered its demolition regardless. The site was replaced by an extension of the Kitchen Garden wall.

By 1983, Cannizaro Park's staff numbered just six full-timers with two extra temporary staff in summertime. In late 1986, Merton's Recreation and Manpower sub-committees were appealing for two extra staff to maintain the park[3], one of them largely concerned with what was now to become an Italian Garden, filling the complete lower half of the Kitchen Garden. In the event, the Italian Garden was created through the Manpower Services Scheme designed to provide employment and skills to young people, and the lower terrace was finished in 1987.

A Council survey in the late 1980s found an estimated 100,000 people a year using Cannizaro Park an average five times each: half a million visits per annum overall. October 1987 saw the great storm uprooting millions of trees across the south of England, including many in Cannizaro. But it also saw the park secure English Heritage registration at Grade II* status, a significant recognition of its importance not just in Wimbledon but London as a whole. There was no shortage of planning for the future, including further development of the Italian Garden. This was to be formal with the upper area maintained temporarily as a grassy area for picnics while the lower terrace had its four beds of fine turf complemented by training of climbing plants on the pergola. Although a hedge of *leylandii* was created between these two sections of the former Kitchen Garden, its walls and gates at each end assumed a common identity for the whole two and half acres. Since the Kitchen Garden had first appeared on maps of the estate dating right back to 1746, this was effectively the very heart of the historic park.

But Merton's ability to commit the necessary funds for a grand new garden design, followed by the maintenance required, was another matter. This simply mirrored a national trend. In October 1999, an all-party House of

Commons committee report[4] estimated a drop of £100 million in parks spending countrywide over the previous eight years. Under-funding of parks of all kinds, including historic ones, was having cumulative effects which led to dereliction and further decline as delayed repairs and maintenance simply added to costs.

Cannizaro Park's ever falling number of staff epitomised the national problem of disappearing park-keepers and inadequate resources as local authorities reduced their budgets or tried to spread them ever more thinly to meet other priorities. This brought vandalism and neglect of historic ornamental features to many parks. The report also said: "We are appalled by English Heritage's neglect of parks and other designed landscapes. Its expenditure and commitment of staff have been derisory."

Grade II* registration was no protection. It was the start of yet another chapter in Cannizaro's evolving story.

NOTES

1. Programme for Wimbledon's Charter Jubilee Celebrations garden party
2. Notes 1999 from Dennis Robbins, Cannizaro gardener 1942 and 1953-66. (ms in Wimbledon Museum of Local History)
3. London Borough of Merton Recreation Executive Sub-Committee, 19th November and Manpower Sub-Committee, 3rd December 1986
4. HOC Environment, Transport and Regional Affairs Committee 20th report Town and Country Parks. Vol 1, 27th Oct 1999

# Chapter 6: Art shows and festival fun

The early years of public ownership saw few large events in Cannizaro Park. It was maintained as a haven of peace and tranquillity, consistent with the use of Cannizaro House as a home for the elderly and the gardens as a horticultural base supplying plants for public displays.

Ball games were not allowed because of the threat they posed to the park's many rare trees and shrubs. Dogs were kept on leads. Fences with neighbouring residential properties were maintained. Development of the Azalea Dell, Herbaceous Border and Heather Garden and construction of the Aviary and the Belvedere were consistent with this policy of long term conservation. Apart from maintenance, park duty for staff in the spring would mainly consist of keeping an eye on the public to stop purloining of camellia flowers for buttonholes and picking of bunches of daffodils.

Merton Council minutes for the 1960s and early 70s show the sort of events permitted in the park. In June 1967 a fete to raise funds for a cardiac monitoring unit at a local hospital. In April 1968 filming by a production company followed by a small donation to the Gardeners Benevolent Fund. An annual Strawberry Tea and Grand Fair organised for a few years by a youth association.

**Visual arts link since Lyde Browne's day**

In May 1974 the park closed for a day to allow the holding of a "Cremorne Gardens" style event during the Merton Festival. This included music, refreshments, a bar and a small antiques fair. It was allowed as a cost-free event to the Council. Also permitted was a "Wombles burrow", open over the spring bank holiday.

Nevertheless, Cannizaro has been associated with visual art since Lyde Browne kept his classical sculptures there in the mid $18^{th}$ century. Later residents too showed interest in paintings and representational work of various forms. An engraving of Warren House made in 1801 followed the common practice at the time of preserving such country houses on paper long before the arrival of photography.[1]

Furthermore, the historic association of the house with music since the days of the Duchess of Cannizzaro provided good reason to continue that tradition, even though the extent of reconstruction since the fire in 1900 ruled out English Heritage listing of the building itself as opposed to the gardens.

From 1948, Cannizaro House was a home for elderly people. However, its cultural significance was still fully appreciated. In January 1951 the Wimbledon Town Clerk provided 15 photographs of works of art from the house for keeping at Wimbledon Library.

Four circular paintings of children in carved frames from the main gallery on the first floor, were thought to be the work of 18th century artist Angelica Kauffmann (1741-1807) who also worked at the nearby Lauriston House, one time home of William Wilberforce. Also attributed to Kauffmann above the ground floor was a circular ceiling work in oil, moulded in plaster. The drawing room contained a white marble mantel with bold bas relief representation of the legendary Androcles and the lion, reputed to have characteristics of the neoclassical architect and designer Robert Adam (1728-92). Wilson had brought this from Roehampton House. The ground floor also had period mahogany folding doors, while a wooden mantel dated $c1600$ and carved oak panelling could be found on the first floor.

When the old folks' home closed in 1977 because of stricter fire regulations, the opportunity arose for restoration of the long-standing link between Cannizaro House and the arts. Merton Council approached the John Evelyn Society with a view to moving its Museum of Local History into the building as part of a new arts centre.[2] The Society was eager to co-operate and as its members included a number of architects and designers, it was well placed to assist.

Merton's Borough Plan at the time showed this as a commitment and the Society made full use of the house as concerts, exhibitions and craft fairs were all staged there. In May 1980 the arts centre was officially declared open as Prince Michael of Kent opened a major exhibition of the work of sculptor David Wynne. An annual three-week arts season was proposed from May 1981.

But the Council was simultaneously negotiating the sale of Cannizaro House to developers. An assurance was given at a public enquiry that "the cultural use of the building would never be lost" and the John Evelyn Society came up with a scheme to retain at least the central part for the arts centre. The Cannizaro Trust was established which planned to raise £300,000 to equip it, with an undertaking to back the running costs for the next century. Merton rejected the plan.

The John Evelyn Society was renamed the Wimbledon Society in 1982 and continued its campaign for a Cannizaro House cultural centre. Despite this, the *Wimbledon News* reported on 14th January 1983 that the house was to be sold off for £750,000. It was to be closed to the public and turned into an office block with cultural or recreational facilities dropped altogether. The paper said: "Both Merton's Planning Committee and Conservation Areas Advisory Committee were strongly opposed to using Cannizaro purely for offices, yet Merton's full Council meeting overturned Planning's decision and voted to sell the house on a 125-year lease for around £750,000."

The veteran local politician Sir Cyril Black (1902-91) who had been involved in the original purchase of Cannizaro and served as Wimbledon's MP from 1950-70, was quoted as saying: "It is very sad it is to be used in such a way." As it turned out, that sale failed to go ahead but it was clear which way Merton Council was thinking.

The arts centre faded and for a few years Cannizaro House was allowed to deteriorate physically, used only for the occasional antiques show, cultural or social event. Merton finally sold it in 1985 on a 125-year lease to Thistle Hotels, part of the Scottish & Newcastle Breweries Group.

A permanent exhibition room was promised for paintings and crafts. Chris Cole, Thistle's director of development wrote: "Thistle Hotels will provide a grant of £5000 per annum in order to assist in the payment of fees for artists who perform at the house at concerts that will be arranged by Merton Arts Council. I am sure that the Wimbledon Society and the Cannizaro Trust will also have the opportunity of putting forward ideas as to how the grant can be used during the year. It is certainly our wish to encourage cultural activities in the house and I am sure that as a result of the grant, more rather than less activity will take place after the hotel is opened."

The company spent £3.7 million on a major refurbishment, added an extra wing to the building, and opened Cannizaro House as "London's first country house hotel" in spring 1987. It had 55 bedrooms and suites, three small banqueting suits, and a restaurant seating 60. The first managers were Pierre and Edina Roth who moved to Wimbledon from the prestigious Palais

Schwarzenberg in Vienna and sought to attract an extremely exclusive clientele.

This might have suited the Baron von Neumann and the Duchess of Cannizzaro's other eminent guests 150 years earlier but it soon became apparent that the hotel's 20$^{th}$ century suburban customers didn't quite match the marketing profile. Management styles and prices were adapted accordingly under successive general managers. By the time Cannizaro House was offered for sale by the then owner, Bridgehouse Hotels, for £20 million in June 2008, it had become a profitable 46-bedroom, four-star hotel specialising in weddings, conferences, and the hosting of tennis stars during Wimbledon Fortnight each summer.

**Art in the park**

The conversion reduced opportunities to use Cannizaro House for art exhibitions although some events have taken place in subsequent years and art works are used for decoration. However that has not affected the park's own longstanding links with the arts. Unlike the house, the park has enjoyed English Heritage Grade II* registration since 1987 and the additional Grade II listing of the marble statue of Diana and the Fawn in 1988 emphasised its heritage. Other permanent features include the Belvedere, created 1980-81 and originally graced by classical style stone urns atop its columns, and Hilda Seligman's bust of Haile Selassie.

Wimbledon School (later College) of Art held its first open air sculpture exhibition in Cannizaro Park in May-June 1978 for four weeks. This was arranged by Glynn Williams, principal lecturer in sculpture from 1976-90 but it set a tradition that has continued in one form or another ever since. Soon after taking over in the late 1940s, Wimbledon Council had even offered Cannizaro House itself to the art school as its base. This had been turned down as the school had only moved into its premises in Merton Park as recently as 1939. However by the 1980s it had taken over redundant potting sheds in the old Kitchen Garden, converting them to studios for students.

That lasted until 2001 and Merton afterwards leased the studios to the arts group ACAVA for low-cost rentals to local professional artists in return for occasional public open days and educational projects. Today the artists work in various media, including ceramics, painting and sculpture. Up to half a dozen at a time rent the studios and their work is often inspired by their beautiful surroundings.

The early years of Wimbledon School of Art's annual exhibition reflected Glynn Williams' speciality in figurative carving, using stone, wood, plaster and concrete. Especially memorable pieces during the 1980s and early 90s included a Mini car on gigantic legs, a gigantic wooden figure pointing towards the sky, and what appeared to be a climbing frame but actually represented the different lines of the London Underground.

Among sculptors who worked with Williams at the school was Richard Rome, later the creator of Cannizaro's Millennium Fountain. Today this remarkable bronze work remains as a tribute to the great monumental style of the early shows, even though few of the temporary exhibits then could have matched its ability to mature with the years. However, it shares with them an ability to arouse strong feelings either of support or hostility among visitors.

After Williams left Wimbledon to become professor of sculpture at the Royal College of Art – later joined by Rome among others – Cannizaro's annual exhibition changed beyond recognition. Monumental pieces gave way to broadened notions of sculpture and less concentration on public statements. Although The Oak and the Mistletoe, a naturalistic stone piece, has been in place permanently near the south lawn since 1993, conceptual and performance art have replaced the more common abstract pieces, often no longer arousing strong emotions but simply blending in with the shapes, colours, light and transitory nature of the park's seasonal attractions.

*Art in the Park: illustrations on following pages:*

*Page 69 (opposite): The first Cannizaro Park Festival was in July 1989*

*Page 70: Top left : Steve Hutton's "When Mutton was on the Menu" (2006)*

*Top right: "Tree Dressing" (2003)*

*Middle left: Trees Reflected (2006)*

*Middle right: Jon Griffiths' Cabin (2004)*

*Bottom left: Martin Newth's "Solar Cinema" (2007)*

*Bottom right : "David Attenborough" finds a rare plant (2009)*

looking up at
the blue sky

AN OPEN-AIR THEATRE SEASON IN
CANNIZARO PARK
DREAMMAKERS PRESENT
THE COUNTRY WIFE
by WILLIAM WYCHERLEY
A MIDSUMMER NIGHT'S DREAM
by WILLIAM SHAKESPEARE
THE MARRIAGE OF FIGARO
by MOZART
JULY 27~AUG 1
AUG 3~AUG 15
AUG 18~AUG 22
BOX OFFICE:
Tel: 081-540 0362
SUNDAY AUG 9th
GEORGE MELLY
and JOHN CHILTERN'S
FEETWARMERS
SUNDAY AUG 23rd
RALPH McTELL
AND GUESTS

CANNIZARO PARK
OPEN-AIR THEATRE
SEASON 1995
CLASSIC ENTERTAINMENT
IN A UNIQUE LOCATION!
THE MUSIC OF THE TSARS
SUNDAY LUNCHTIME JAZZ
THE BLUES BAND
THE IMPORTANCE OF BEING EARNEST
JONGLEURS COMEDY NIGHT
A MIDSUMMER NIGHT'S DREAM
GEORGE MELLY
THE MAGIC FLUTE
LA BOHEME
ROMEO & JULIET
HINGE & BRACKET
THE BOYFRIEND
KENNY BALL
15 JULY - 20 AUGUST
BOX OFFICE 0181 540 0362

r. j. williamson COMPANY
the Cannizaro Park
WIMBLEDON OPEN
THEATRE FESTIVAL
10th July
8th
Circus
Opera
Musicals
Children's Events
Shakespeare
Concerts
Comedy
Jazz

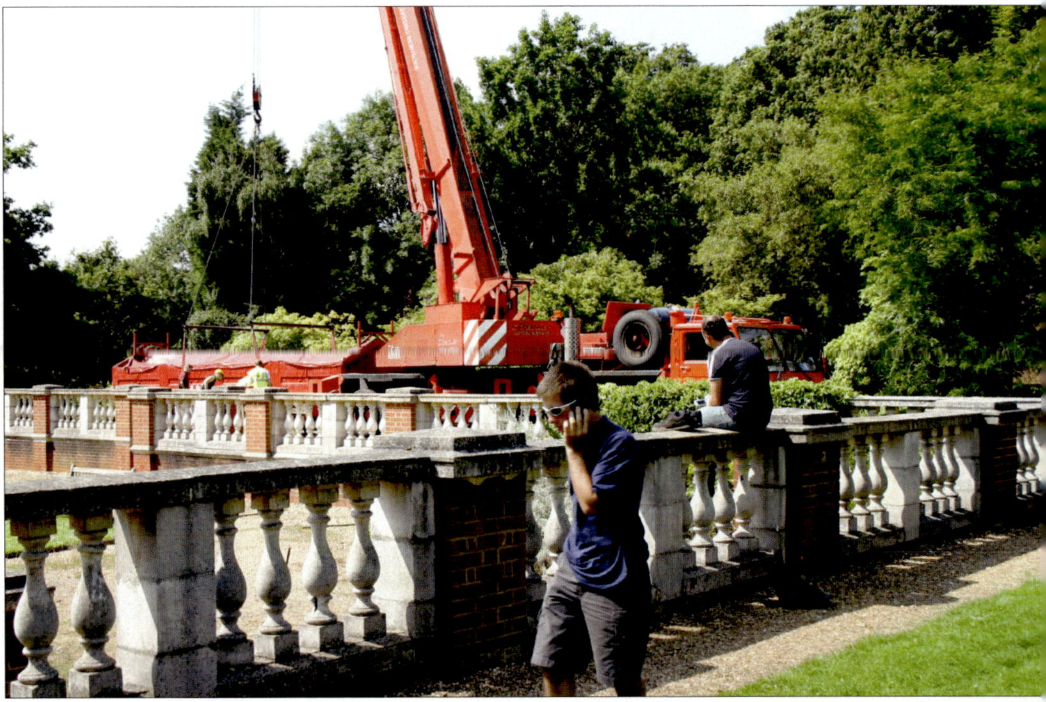

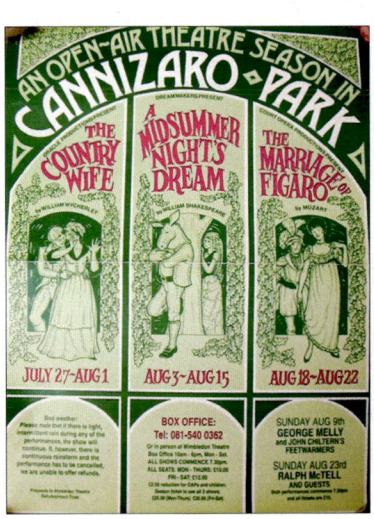

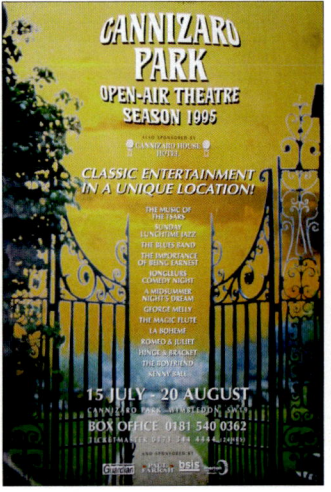

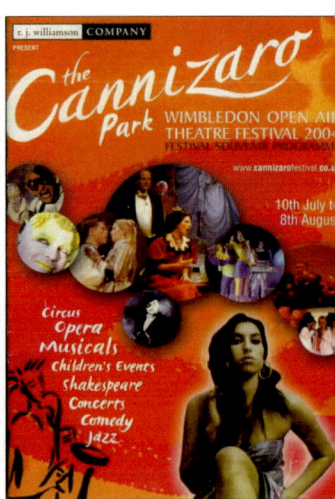

*Art in the Park: illustrations on previous pages:*

Page 71: Top left upper: "Offerings to the Tree Spirit" (2009)

Top left lower: Gingerbread George W Bush (2005)

Top right : Christine Macallan's "Gift Shared" (2006)

Bottom: Mediterranean Garden in Cannizaro Park (2005)
     by Kath Montagu of ACAVA

Page 73: Scenes and posters from the open air festival

Top: Preparing the festival infrastructure in the Italian Garden

Bottom left: 1992 Festival poster

Bottom centre: 1995 Festival poster

Bottom right: 2004 Festival poster

Today, the annual show, PARK, continues each May but has been reduced to a single weekend. Although most of its content is entirely transient, an exception was Toby Christian's 2005 contribution, the two-stage cleaning of Diana and the Fawn, a cooperative project with partners beyond the school. The exhibition itself that year took the title "Skulpcha". Explaining its emphasis on transience, Sally Shaw, the college's Curator, said its most striking feature was "the predominance of works that result in no permanent objects at all". Sculpture existed in a manipulation of time and place rather than physical materials.

Other works included Steve Wright's gingerbread models of President George W Bush suspended from a tree by Connoisseurs' Corner; Ambrosine Allen's "Proposals for the End of the World", a continual experiment by the Belvedere in wood and found objects; and Karolina Honkajuuri's "Tea Party with My Monkey", performed with a crochet primate.

The exhibition has since become a show for all students with a selected number chosen by the organisers from proposals submitted. Wimbledon College of Art now invites other institutions to join its Cannizaro show and adopts particular themes. In 2009 this involved expressions of myth and reality to present extraordinary concepts such as the discovery of a new tropical bird species or polar bears in the park.

**Individual exhibitions**

Separately from the college, Cannizaro Park has also hosted a series of individual arts events in recent years. Several of these were arranged by Art Works in Wimbledon, a local specialist organiser. In winter 2003, conceptual artist Keith Wilson presented three galvanised steel structures in the park under the collective title "Liberty". Funded by The Henry Moore Foundation and the Arts Council of England, they were modern representations of the old livestock pound across the Common from Cannizaro.

Keith Wilson's contradictory title for structures designed to constrain livestock invited comparison between these and the restrictions of modern streets where our own instincts to roam were constrained by the barriers between pedestrians and modern traffic. Set in the park landscape, the structures became public objects to be looked at, sat or leant on, played around, entered and left. Their role as sculptures became ambiguous as they took on an everyday function, like existing park furniture.

In 2004, artist Jon Griffiths built a cabin in the woodland of Cannizaro as a temporary living space touching on the desire to get away from it all by living on the land. For one week, he recalled the 19$^{th}$-century American man of letters, Henry David Thoreau, who lived for two years in a cabin in rural Massachusetts to "engage with the essential facts of life". In 2007-8, Art Works in Wimbledon presented SOLAR Cinema, Martin Newth's seasonal camera obscura, set up for a couple of days in each of the natural seasons. This threw a new light on images of different areas of the park from within a darkened marquee. Instead of freezing the image like a conventional camera, the projection framed a section of the park inverted within the screen.

Among the most memorable of all the events were exhibitions of Zimbabwean sculptures held in the Italian Garden for three weeks each summer from 2005-7. Every year, visiting sculptors exhibited over 100 representational works in springstone, opal stone, butterjade and other natural materials from their country. Free carving workshops were provided for local youngsters. A commercial as well as an artistic event, these shows were an opportunity to appreciate the remarkable quality of work coming out of one of the world's most troubled countries. Despite the sad vandalism that temporarily set back the first show, the contrast between events in Zimbabwe and Cannizaro's normally tranquil surroundings could hardly have been more marked.

*Zimbabwean sculpture show in the Italian Garden (2005)*
*"Bathing Sheeba" (dolomite) by Gregory Mutasa and*
*"Collecting Firewood" (opal stone) by Taylor Nkomo.*

## Music, drama and popular entertainment

Visual art has its place but open air theatre also returned to Cannizaro in June 1979 when the Acorn Childrens Theatre Trust staged two evening performances of Shakespeare's "A Midsummer Night's Dream". It was nearly a century since Mrs Schuster's staging in the gardens of "Fair Rosamund" with her royal and other guests in the audience. But as then, the grounds provided an atmospheric setting and set the scene for all that was to follow in terms of summer festivals.

By 1988, after a number of open air concerts had been held in the park over the years, Merton Arts Council decided to use Cannizaro Park for a fully fledged four-day arts festival with events both in the Italian Garden and elsewhere. It would be held in summer 1989.

The first year saw a one-week event with "A Midsummer Night's Dream" once again the key production and free musical performances to draw public interest. There were also children's events and the festival spread through different areas of the park. It proved a popular combination. The stage was set for an annual festival which would soon grow first to two weeks and then a full month. Shakespeare plays, opera and ballet performed against the elements would bring an extra dimension to Cannizaro Park's cultural identity.

In 1990, Michael Lyas, manager of Wimbledon Theatre, saw an opportunity for summer performances in Cannizaro Park at a time when the theatre itself was closed for refurbishment. Although he had no experience of open air productions, he saw the Italian Garden as an ideal location. Yet again it was "A Midsummer Night's Dream" that was selected and Lyas persuaded local actor Leo Dolan to partner him in a new company Dream Makers Ltd, casting and directing the play while he created the theatre and handled the administration. Funding was provided by Dream Makers while Merton took 10% of any profit or the same amount of any loss. Estate agency Robert Holmes & Co was among the local sponsors.

For Lyas it was the beginning of a seven-year love affair with what became the Cannizaro Park Open Air Theatre Season but everything he took for granted in a normal theatre had to be sourced – from electricity to toilet rolls and from dressing rooms to tickets.

His first year went well enough to encourage expansion of the season in 1991 to four weeks. This time it included a production of "The Country Wife", another two weeks of "A Midsummer Night's Dream" and "The Marriage of Figaro", as well as popular concerts with performances by jazz singer George Melly and folk artist Ralph McTell. Although the season lost money, Lyas carried on for the next five years, expanding the season to five weeks, putting on many more and varied one night stands, and introducing the especially popular Sunday lunchtime jazz sessions.

The noise of aircraft overhead was a distraction but the weather was generally acceptable and in seven years the organisers only had to cancel about eight shows out of nearly 400. Perhaps most memorable of these was a performance of "Dracula" when the actor playing the Count made his first entrance by jumping up on to a wall just as there was the most enormous flash of lightning and crash of thunder. Lyas heard an audience member ask: "How did they do that?".

He has many abiding memories of those festivals. They include the theft of the lighting board on the eve of the first night; members of the audience (including those in wheelchairs) dancing with the cast of "The Pirates of Penzance" at the end of the show; Puck being framed exactly by an enormous (real) full moon at the end of "A Midsummer Night's Dream"; and the sound of Bizet's "Pearl Fishers" duet floating magically on the breeze in outlying areas of the park. Audiences chanced the elements and often enjoyed glorious warm evenings in idyllic surroundings as the sun set and music or drama ensured a feel-good experience.

Unfortunately, the festival's financial success was never assured. Lyas hoped Merton would provide a grant to help him take the festival to another level but instead the Council demanded a large rent for future events. In 1997 after eight years of trying to match triumphs on stage with profits behind the scenes, he left Wimbledon to run the Maddermarket Theatre in Norwich.

Merton Council had to look elsewhere for organisers to keep the festival going. It turned in 1989 to Opera Box, a Welsh touring company founded by Brendan Wheatley and Bridget Gill to specialise in outdoor performances of opera and theatre at English Heritage sites. The new partnership worked well and the company also operated creative opera residencies with pupils from two Merton schools performing in a production of "Carmen".

However, financial questions intervened and the partnership ended in 2002 when the Wimbledon Civic Theatre Trust took over the running of the festival. Just a year later the trust announced its own financial difficulties. In June 2003 a bid by Merton to rescue the festival failed late in the day. It was to have run from 13th July to 10th August but despite intervention by the Ambassador Theatre Group, then in the process of taking over management of Wimbledon Theatre, and pledges of sponsorship, Merton Council said "significant hurdles" remained.

Keith Davis, the Council's director of customer services and development, said it was difficult to secure companies that would supply equipment, skilled staff, quality performers, goods and other services but the spirit of the festival was alive and well and it would be back. So it proved.

The music and spectacle returned with the 13th festival managed this time by another open air theatre specialist, Robert Williamson. The festival was a great success with "Mama Mia" selling out immediately, daytime workshops, and Sunday jazz bringing in some 16,000 festival goers. Big names included singer Amy Winehouse and ballet dancer Wayne Sleep.

But unsettled weather still hit bookings and although plans started for another month-long event in 2005 the upbeat mood couldn't hide the continuing uncertainty. Even the Friends of Cannizaro Park special evening which had been very successful in earlier years had shown a marked decline. Its choice of Gilbert & Sullivan songs for the specially discounted performance attracted only 40 members. Robert Williamson's company folded at the last minute, hit by financial difficulties elsewhere. Keen to avoid another lost year, Merton stepped in and organised the 2005 festival itself.

It was not prepared to do the same in 2006. This time Robert Holmes & Co and PMB Holdings, both sponsors of previous festivals, decided to establish a consortium of 25 local businesses to fund the event over an agreed three-year period and test the long-term viability of the festival. Cannizaro Event Ltd was set up to raise the necessary funds. It contracted with Merton to run the 2006 festival with an option to do the same for the next two years. The Ambassador Theatre Group provided an event manager and handled the ticketing.

**Three-year experiment**

The firm Maximum Exposure was taken on to produce the programme. It also organised open air infrastructure which for the first time included covered seating for 600 people. The event was held from 22$^{nd}$ July to 16$^{th}$ August back in the Italian Garden after a one-year switch to the top end of the old Kitchen Garden.

From 2006-8 the renamed Wimbledon Cannizaro Festival was run by the Ambassador Theatre Group while Cannizaro Event Ltd raised the funds. Each festival ran for two weeks and the costs rose as covered stands and generally more expensive infrastructure were matched by high price performers. Lunchtime jazz was dropped while Shakespeare and opera were overshadowed or replaced by nostalgic rock music and stand up comedy. But despite the changes and some sell-out performances the sponsors continued to lose money, culminating in an overall loss in 2008 of £139,000.[3]

Some problems seemed insurmountable. Timing was one. The festival had to be held at the start of the school holidays in the week following the end of Wimbledon tennis fortnight. As Merton was providing the infrastructure, some of this had to be transferred directly from the All-England ground to Cannizaro, affecting the festival's logistics.

In 2008 moreover, the festival was brought forward to the Friday after the championships ended rather than Saturday as in the past, reducing set-up time in a bid to maximise revenues. Holding the event any later would have put it in the depths of the school holidays when many potential customers would be away. Earlier than Wimbledon tennis fortnight would be impossible, competing with Wimbledon Theatre's own season.

Cannizaro Park's lack of parking space was also believed to be a disadvantage. Drivers to the festival either had to fill neighbouring streets – to the annoyance of residents – or park further away in controlled zones. Parking on the Common was not an option since events in Cannizaro Park were ineligible for this concession under the regulations, unlike those on the Common itself.

Sponsorship was needed but after years of nil returns a way had to be found to defray costs to attract future investors. Audience sizes in the park were also limited by licence to 1000 per performance so there would always be a ceiling on profits from ticket sales unless costs were reduced.

Merton Council rejected the sponsors' suggestion that the event be renamed simply the Wimbledon Festival in order to draw audiences from further afield as it was felt outsiders might be unfamiliar with Cannizaro Park. The vagaries of the weather also continued notwithstanding the covered seating. Many potential ticket buyers would wait until very late before making their un-refundable purchases.

Cannizaro Event Ltd considered possible changes to make it profitable for investors, even though it was too late for 2009. Could it be biennial rather than annual? Were the acts right? Why didn't local residents support the festival come what may? Was inadequate marketing to blame? The New Wimbledon Theatre blamed economic recession for the cancellation in 2009 and hoped enough investment could be drawn for a return of the festival in 2010 but this was clearly going to be an uphill struggle.

Comedy had proved most popular in recent years, drawing greater audiences than the Shakespeare or operatic performances of earlier festivals. Jimmy Carr, Bill Bailey, Jo Brand and Paul Merton were all big stars. Other entertainers such as Elkie Brooks, tribute bands performing shows like "Mamma Mia" and "We Will Rock You", and Elvis Presley impersonators had all attracted sell-out audiences. But the rock star Suzi Quatro had only achieved a 26% attendance, tenor Aled Jones only 40%, and even the great jazz player and radio star Humphrey Lyttelton just 54% at one of his last performances. Big names meant big costs and they simply didn't match the returns. Young performers from the Brits School had proved successful without the fees required by big stars. Might they provide a feasible alternative for cheaper staging of festivals in future?

Cannizaro's ability to please as a venue for arts and entertainment is beyond doubt. Just how that squares with the practicalities of funding and organising such events is a different matter. Merton Council, while keen to retain the festival, has always been reluctant to underwrite it on behalf of local taxpayers.

Despite all, yet another event management company, BSL, came forward in March 2010 with plans for a 14-night festival in the summer, selling tickets via the Ambassador Theatre box office. Once again, comedy evenings, tribute bands and popular jazz were on offer.

How it would all pan out in the longer term remained to be seen.

NOTES

1. Warren House entrance, 26$^{th}$ May 1801, by an unknown artist. Wimbledon Society Museum of Local History
2. Wimbledon Society Centenary Souvenir, 2003
3. Time & Leisure, July 2009

# Chapter 7: Keeping the magic alive

Since 1996, the Friends of Cannizaro Park have worked with Merton Council and other partners to protect the legacy of the gardens for the future. It is an impressive success story and it continues today. With a membership of more than 500, some of whom live far from the park, the Friends have played a crucial role. The gardening staff have been even more important, of course, but it could not have been achieved without close cooperation between the group and Merton officials, Cannizaro House Hotel, Wimbledon College of Art, festival organisers, local and visiting artists, schools, horticulturalists, naturalists, tree experts, historians, other park supporters groups, the police, and ultimately the general public.

Thousands of pounds have been raised and spent on plants, restorations, and promotional activities. Plants in the main entrance beds, the terrace beds beside the hotel, the new Herb Garden, the Water Garden, the Iris Beds, the Azalea Dell and the Sunken Garden have all had Friends' involvement. The notice-boards, cycle racks, signposts, bird and bat boxes, pond pump and Herb Garden benches were all funded or planned by the Friends. The iconic Millennium Fountain was commissioned by them and the historic statues of Diana and Haile Selassie restored with their support.

Every year the group has arranged lectures by professional experts, guided tours and other activities, both for members and other visitors to the park. Children's events have been designed to show the next generation why Cannizaro's plants and wildlife are so precious and in need of care. Yet the Friends of Cannizaro Park originally came into being because of disagreement over the park, not cooperation.

On 18th June 1996 some 40 neighbours of Cannizaro Park attended a special meeting of the Wimbledon Common West Residents Association at the Study School in Camp Road. The chairman told the audience of his group's efforts over the previous six months to convince Merton councillors that their new cost-saving policy of leaving Cannizaro Park unlocked overnight was inviting a plague of crime.

Chris Mountford, client and technical manager with Merton's Education & Leisure Department, explained that the Council had decided to stop locking all of its 35 parks overnight in April 1995 and would save £70,000 a year as a result. The answer for Cannizaro - and other parks - was for local volunteers to set up Friends groups which would unlock the entrances themselves each morning. If Cannizaro had such volunteers, Merton staff would lock gates each evening.

Eveline Hastings, a local professional artist and leader of a sub-committee of the residents association, said the Council had refused to consider Cannizaro's Grade II* registration and vulnerable horticultural collection as sufficient justification to distinguish it from any other park in the borough. Some people living adjacent to the gardens had already begun unlocking the gates informally each morning as Chris Mountford had suggested but if formed, a Friends of Cannizaro Park group would do more than just that. Its role would be to help preserve the beauty as well as the safety of the gardens after years of declining maintenance because of Merton's cost cuts. In view of Cannizaro's special importance, members would be recruited far more widely than just those living nearby.

*Opposite page: Spring and summer scenes in Cannizaro Park*

*Page 84:*

*Top left: Friends of Cannizaro Park join Merton staff to replant the Water Garden in 2006*

*Top right: Haile Selassie's family celebrate his statue's restoration in 2005*

*Middle left: Anthony Gardiner talks on herbs at Cannizaro House*

*Middle right: The Aviary before recent replanting*

*Bottom left: Diana during the cleaning process*

*Bottom right: The Millennium Fountain is prepared at the artist's studio before installation in 2001*

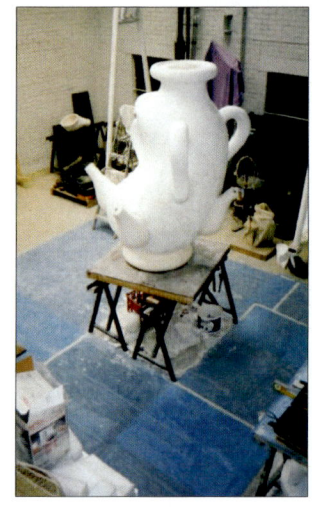

Page 85:

Top: Friends of Cannizaro Park plant stand at the Wimbledon Village Fair, 2005

Middle left : Cycle racks at the main entrance

Middle right: Herb Garden, 2009

Bottom left : Magnolia Soulangeana

Bottom right: Dave Lofthouse explains the workings of nature

Opposite page: Two views of the Italian Garden

A resolution to form such a group was passed by the meeting and Eveline Hastings was elected to the chair. Annual subscription was to be £5 and the first official meeting of the Friends Executive Committee followed on 20th November. The group's objectives were formally adopted as follows: "To ensure Cannizaro Park's continuation as a Grade II* listed garden; support maintenance by Merton in the best possible condition; require continuing security for the garden, both day and night; encourage a balance between the needs and wishes of those who enjoy the garden in a variety of ways with its protected status; protect the garden's flora, fauna and structures; and encourage responsibility in their appreciation and enjoyment."

A constitution was adopted at the first Annual General Meeting on 28th June 1997. Apart from a permanent arrangement for locking of the park gates overnight, the priorities were new notice-boards at the main and rear entrances and replanting of the iris beds near Connoisseurs Corner. Annual improvements to the park were to be agreed in future with Merton.

The iris beds were quickly replanted in July 1997 by volunteers advised by specialist Mary Tubbs and after lengthy discussions with Merton, the new notice-boards were eventually installed in June 1998.

Fund-raising projects were also organised to replace the park's vandalised deckchairs with ten new ones and contribute towards new cycle racks at the main entrance. The group also discussed the annual sculpture exhibition with Wimbledon School of Art because of concerns about exhibits damaging the lawns. Tours of the gardens were organised for supporters and from 1998, discounts on tickets for the open air festival were arranged for members.

Right from the start the group took a proactive approach towards ensuring its objectives were met. Grant applications were investigated to pay for more substantial improvements to the park following the years of decline. Seeking the experience of others, the well established Friends of Holland Park group in West London was consulted on how to secure big increases in both funds and membership. Representatives came to meet the Friends Committee.

The general manager of Cannizaro House Hotel was a Friends Committee member at the start but left in September 1998. Henceforth the Friends and the hotel would work alongside each other, cooperating on common interests but without compromising their own priorities.

Since transforming the building into a country house hotel in 1987, Thistle had always marketed it with the lawns and Sunken Garden as an exclusive location to match the hotel itself. Although its lease extended no further than the back terrace, this was natural enough as those were the areas of the park used most by paying guests, especially at weddings and other functions. While the Friends prioritised the trees, plants, wildlife and artworks that justified the park's Grade II* registration, the hotel had its business to run. There were sometimes disagreements but these were always settled quickly. An early example was the hotel's effort to remove one of the park's prize trees, a superb mature *Magnolia delavayi* thought to be obstructing a window view. The Friends protested and the tree stayed. It is there to this day.

For several years the group's Annual General Meetings were held elsewhere, either at Eagle House in the village or at Wimbledon Golf Club. But from 2005 onwards, the Friends and successive hotel managements have worked well together. Two group events a year are always held there and a series of fund-raising dinner dances have helped boost resources for spending on the park and the group's profile in the local community.

**Growth and long term effectiveness**

By 1999, after enjoying a steady growth in membership and recognition, the Friends of Cannizaro Park were able to organise three much bigger projects than hitherto. These were a 50$^{th}$ anniversary celebration of public ownership and access; a major restoration of the ever popular but overgrown Azalea Dell; and the creation of a dramatic new fountain near the main entrance. Each of these would have lasting effects for the park. (Unlike the deckchairs which soon suffered the fate of their predecessors and were not replaced).

Most immediate was the 50th anniversary celebration of the opening of Cannizaro Park itself. This took place on 29th April 1999. Merton Council had rejected a bid for funding but the Friends achieved their first big triumph with a marquee on the main lawn for four days. This hosted refreshments and a raffle, and dispensed publicity material about the park, supported by the Wimbledon Society. Morris dancers provided entertainment and Mrs Connie Curry, a lifelong neighbour of Cannizaro since 1914 and authoress of a popular local history book,[1] planted a commemorative *Nyssa sylvatica* (tupelo) tree beside the Aviary.

Two booklets went on sale with the authors signing copies. Published by the Friends especially for the anniversary, these covered the horticulture, history and wildlife of the park. One was partly written by James Berry who described himself as a former "honorary foreman". In fact, as deputy director of Merton's Recreation and Arts Department until 1985, he had managed Cannizaro Park over many years, masterminding the creation or restoration of many of its major features. No-one knew the gardens in greater detail or better appreciated the work that had gone into them.

The other booklet was the work of Tony Drakeford, probably Wimbledon's best known naturalist and an elected conservator of Wimbledon and Putney Commons. He had already led the first of a series of guided walks in the park in autumn 1998 and would continue to do so on behalf of the Friends in following years.

Long-term book sales apart, the anniversary made £700 profit towards general activities. But this was a small sum compared to the cost of the group's next triumph, the pruning and replanting of the Azalea Dell for which the group raised £3000 through determined campaigning. The project lasted throughout 1999 and by April 2000 the job was done, with 450 new azaleas in place and funded by the Friends. By then a still bigger project was on the horizon.

In January 1999, Martin Holman, a professional arts organiser, joined the Committee, bringing both his expertise in securing of grants for art projects and a notably higher profile for the Friends as a group. In October, a competition was launched to commission an artist who would create and install a new fountain near the main entrance. This would replace one that had suffered repeated vandalism. The commission was worth £50,000 and the brief aimed to attract applicants from as wide a range of backgrounds as possible. The selection criteria stressed safety, durability and suitability but artists also had to respond creatively to the fountain's location as it was the

first view most visitors would have on arriving at the park.
The water feature was intended to please and fascinate children in particular. The Friends wanted it to be unique to Cannizaro, robust, insurable against public liability, easy to care for, and with a lifespan of at least 30 years. The commission was awarded by the Constance Fund, a body specialising in new sculpture for public parks, and the project was administered jointly by the Friends, the Royal Society of British Sculptors and Merton Council.

A shortlist of three proposals was chosen from among 60 applications and each was exhibited at Wimbledon Library in March 2000. The winner, Richard Rome, was a former teacher at Wimbledon School of Art. On 27th January 2001, the new Millennium Fountain was formally inaugurated by Sir Christopher Frayling, rector of the Royal College of Art, at a ceremony attended by over 100 Friends and guests. Mayor Ian Munn took possession of the work for Merton and the fountain was described as either a giant classical style urn or a multi-spouted teapot reminiscent of Alice in Wonderland. Some viewers hated it, many more loved it and it has since become a unique feature of Cannizaro Park.

As each of the three big projects worked its way towards completion, the Friends were equally involved in other initiatives to promote public interest in Cannizaro Park and expand support for its improvement. In November 1999, a Gardeners' Question Time was organised at the hotel, establishing a precedent for an annual event there each winter. Merton's Chris Mountford, Cliff Iles, Dave Lofthouse and James Berry formed a team to answer questions in the format of the BBC radio show.

In subsequent years winter speakers would include Wimbledon historian Richard Milward; gardening writer and broadcaster Caroline Holmes; Hampton Court nursery manager Martin Einchcomb; Ham House head gardener Peter Clark; Director of the Royal Botanic Gardens Sir Peter Crane; snowdrops expert John Grimshaw; and garden historian Jane Gardiner. All proved highly popular with audiences.

Nor was the Friends' lecture programme limited to the winter. Jane Gardiner's husband Anthony, the herb specialist, would be among various speakers at summertime AGMs. Others would include Rod Bugg and Elizabeth Prosser of Wimbledon School of Art; rhododendron expert Sharon Evans from Richmond Park's Isabella Plantation; dendrologist Tony Titchen; Wimbledon Common wildlife liaison officer Dave Haldane; and the organiser of the Zimbabwean sculpture exhibitions, Vivienne Prince.

The Friends also organised guided walks by visiting experts such as Dave Dawson of the London Ecology Unit to complement those by Tony Drakeford, Chris Mountford and Dave Lofthouse. Wimbledon's Polka Theatre for children was brought in to assist with special events for youngsters that combined fun with education about the gardens.

For some years the Friends sold plants and promotional material from their own stall at the Wimbledon Village Fair, helping to raise the group's profile. Special evenings at the open air festival had a more mixed record of success but in August 2001, more than 100 members attended a performance of Puccini's "La Boheme" and this was matched the following year for "West Side Story". From 2004, visits to other gardens were organised, generally following lectures on these by guest speakers. Hampton Court, Ham House and Kew were all featured and there was even a visit to Prince Charles' garden at Highgrove, following a rare invitation there.

Other ventures included production and sale of postcards depicting the park's seasonal colours. In time, a Cannizaro DVD made by independent producer Peter Fison would also have the Friends' endorsement. Regular newsletters were produced to keep members aware of developments in the park and posters produced especially for the new notice-boards. Leaflets were published to support recruitment and a Friends of Cannizaro Park web site was established in 2004 to attract wider interest beyond the membership. It proved highly successful.

**Every aspect of the park**

Membership grew to well over 500 but the ultimate purpose of the Friends was always to see the park's precious features protected or enhanced, however well known the park would become and whatever its year-round visitor level. Some of those features were permanent, some temporary. Rare trees and plants, carefully designed landscapes, the pond, woodland, and artworks all required attention.

The wildlife was generally left to its own devices, although concern was always shown for the large badger sett and in 2005 the Friends installed 15 bird-boxes and 12 bat-boxes to encourage creatures of the air such as tawny owls, kestrels, and the bat species, pipistrelles and noctules. They also paid £1000 for a pump to be installed in the pond to improve oxygen levels for the resident carp and other fish.

A project to identify and label every rare tree in the park proved rather too ambitious. Although dendrologist Tony Titchen was hired in 2003 to help Merton's tree expert Dave Lofthouse identify every species, actually securing and installing all the labels turned out to be beyond the Council's means. Nevertheless, 37 of 250 identified tree species were labelled and the Friends then published a tour guide to them all. This was written by Chris Mountford whose personal knowledge and experience of Cannizaro was invaluable. Newly marked specimens included various oaks, sassafras, sequoias, magnolias, acers, birches, cedars, and the remarkable "double" black pine in the Mediterranean Garden.

The project coincided with new plantings to replace trees that had died. Among new additions were *Fagus sylvatica*, the common beech, and *Tilia henryana*, an unusual lime tree; *Magnolia stellata* and *Acer rubrum* at the top of the Azalea Dell path; *Betula pendula Youngii*, the weeping type, and an oak, *Quercus petraea*, by the lawns; and *Nyssa sylvatica*, a tupelo from North America, towards the Keir Garden. *Magnolia kobus* arrived on the back wall of the Sunken Garden and others included *Paulownia tomentosae, Olea Europaea*, the olive tree, *Morus nigra,* the black mulberry, and a couple of rare American chestnuts, *Aesculus pavia altrosanguinea*, and *Aesculus flava*.

Cannizaro's permanent structures also preoccupied the Friends. When the high wall beside Camp Road was destroyed by a gale in 1999, they pressed Merton for rapid action. It was eventually rebuilt and climbing plants introduced to soften the appearance. In late 2005, the group campaigned for rapid repairs to the Aviary when its base was succumbing to rot. The structure was fully repaired and the birds' home secured. (The residents may have been mightily relieved: squirrels had been gaining access and pilfering their food).

By 2002, the former sheds and storage buildings of the old Kitchen Garden were disused after Wimbledon School of Art had stopped using them as studios. For two years the Friends pressed for clearance of the derelict structures which were clearly undermining the overall appearance of the adjacent pond and Italian Garden. Eventually at the end of 2003, the wreckage was removed and a new contract agreed between Merton and the arts group ACAVA to restore the remaining sheds for use as low rent studios by local professional artists. The Friends made contact immediately with the studios' new residents and helped to publicise their open days to visitors.

**Restoring the artworks**

Each of these permanent structure issues involved extensive discussions between the Friends and Merton. In each case it was the Council that ultimately paid for the repairs but the Millennium Fountain had set a precedent for financial involvement by the Friends too. So it was to be with Cannizaro's other two most prominent artworks, the statues of Diana and the Fawn and Emperor Haile Selassie.

In summer 2000 the Friends had supported planting of a yew hedge behind Diana and the Fawn. With its own Grade II listing, the statue dated back to 1841 and had once stood right outside Cannizaro House. Moved to its present location many years before, by the 1990s its back-lot of garden waste and severe weathering of its surface made it look sadly neglected. The yews, it was hoped, would provide a suitable bower for the nymph.

Unfortunately they failed to establish effectively and by 2005, the statue itself was in an even sorrier state, the plaster at its base badly damaged. Enter Wimbledon School of Art student Toby Christian who appealed to the Friends and Merton together to help him arrange restoration of the statue as his contribution to the annual sculpture show. To the Friends, this was a perfect opportunity. They joined the art school and Merton in paying Toby's costs of hiring the conservation firm Holden's to clean half of the statue for the exhibition weekend itself and then complete the job three weeks later. Diana so became the only lasting feature of the school's "Skulpcha" exhibition that year, emphasising transience. It was a happy outcome, although "transient" seemed hardly appropriate for Cannizaro's oldest established statue. Then again, cleaning would be an ongoing process so perhaps it was. Moreover, by summer 2009 the statue had been vandalised and restoration was needed once more. Diana's perfection really had proven all too transient.

In November 2004, the Friends were approached by Mrs Nancy-Joan Seligman, daughter-in-law of Hilda Seligman, creator of Cannizaro's bust of Haile Selassie. Nancy-Joan still recalled meeting the exiled monarch at a garden party at Lincoln House.

Switched to its current position in 1985, like Diana, the bust was now suffering from years of neglect with hairline cracks and facial damage. Nancy-Joan had offered to pay towards its restoration on behalf of her family. After Diana's transformation the time seemed perfect and the Friends agreed swift joint action with Merton.

*The author with Merton's Mayor after unveiling of the bust of Haile Selassie*

Haile Selassie's restoration, costing around £1000, was again carried out by Holden's. It was followed in October 2005 by a truly historic unveiling ceremony that brought together descendants of Haile Selassie himself; a large number of Rastafarians for whom the late Emperor was a sacred figure; Nancy-Joan and other members of the Seligman family; the Mayor of Merton and other officials; and the Friends of Cannizaro Park. The Ethiopian Embassy didn't respond to an invitation but enquiries about the event were received from as far away as California. With online comments on the event from around the world, Cannizaro Park's profile had been raised to a record high. Whether or not the exiled Emperor ever actually visited the gardens, his role in the Cannizaro story is now assured.

**Clashes over resources**

These were clearly major successes for the Friends but the original reason for the group's establishment continued to cast a shadow. This was the knock-on effect of reduced spending on parks by the Council in order to meet other financial demands. The deteriorating situation of parks nationwide described in the 1999 House of Commons report continued unabated and Merton was no exception.

The report had recognised the growth of voluntary groups like the Friends of Cannizaro Park as a possible way of filling the spending gap by raising funds and securing grants from available sources. In just three years since 1996, the Heritage Lottery Fund had already awarded £117 million to park schemes, becoming the main impetus for action on historic parks. Although such capital schemes assumed local authorities would provide appropriate resources for future maintenance, the HLF was at least starting to switch some of the dependence for major restoration costs away from council tax.

Budget cuts meant ever fewer staff to maintain Cannizaro as a Grade II* registered garden. By the new century, only three gardening staff remained, all sharing their working hours at Cannizaro with other parks. A short-lived ranger service was established to handle security, clear litter and so on but this soon disappeared in one of many staff reorganisations. Merton's pool of staff for all of its parks continued to shrink.

Eveline Hastings retired as Chair of the Friends at the end of 1999 and her successor later wrote to Merton's Leader, Andrew Judge, to protest at a decision to slash another 10% of the parks budget from April 2002. Further staff reorganisation threatened to undermine the Council promise to retain Cannizaro's flagship status, bringing deterioration for the gardens.

The declining budget meant the gradual disappearance of labour-intensive features introduced in earlier years. Those sacrificed included both the Herbaceous Border and the Heather Garden. After nearly 50 years as one of the park's finest features, the Herbaceous Border with its red hot pokers and spectacle of summertime colour disappeared forever in 2002, grassed over for what was originally to be just three years. No trace of it now remains beside the western wall of the Italian Garden.

The Heather Garden had been planted at the lower end of the park beyond Lady Jane's Wood. In 1980 when labour was more plentiful, nearly two acres formerly used as a waste dump and for supplying gravel for pathways were cleared and the heathers planted. In broad sweeps of late summer flowering cultivars, the brightest colours were planted close to the specially built Belvedere at the eastern end. The idea was to magnify the length of the garden from there and create a surprise element for visitors emerging from Lady Jane's Wood. Sadly the plan allowed neither for vandals, who soon knocked over the Belvedere's columns, nor the dryness of the slope which proved too difficult to irrigate. The columns would be restored in time, minus their classical decorations, but the heathers largely died out.

The Friends of Cannizaro Park always argued for alternative planting and indeed a credible replacement for the Heather Garden was proposed by Merton. From 2001, it became the Mediterranean Garden, planted with cistus, stone pines and Corsican black pines, thought more likely to thrive on soil made up of sand and gravel with minimal nutrient content.

The result was mixed. The project needed manpower for completion and this was simply insufficient. In time the Mediterranean Garden reverted to wilderness, the main effort going into creating a zigzag path for disabled visitors which was soon hopelessly eroded by heavy rain. Only in 2009, when the gardeners received voluntary assistance from pupils of King's College School under a special educational project, was it possible to restore the site to anything like the Mediterranean Garden intended.

For years the Friends could do little about this part of the park. It was simply too large for the sort of projects they could afford and required extensive manpower. Their strengths were to contribute publicity and a certain level of funding for improvements. However, they did sometimes intervene directly as with the iris beds in 1997.

In 2003 the Friends both financed and joined the gardeners in replanting the terrace beds in front of the hotel. Daffodils, tulips, New Zealand flax *Phormium, Verbena,* irises, geraniums, *Artemesia,* box balls, roses, *Agapantus, Rudbeckia* and modern grasses such as *Stipa* were all found a place. Three years later in May 2006, the Friends helped Cannizaro's gardeners replant the Wild Garden. This was the area behind the Water Garden cascade which had become totally clogged and was fast disappearing. The Friends paid £6000 for a wider restoration programme in the park of which this was the biggest element. They helped transform the area with more than 40 different species of new plants including azaleas, acers, hydrangeas, *Phormium,* geraniums, irises, *Arum* and hellebors.

The project followed disagreement with Merton over a decision in 2004 to axe all summer bedding plants borough-wide in 2005. The Council was seeking to fill a £12 million deficit and the parks looked a good target. As Cannizaro's Sunken Garden was by far the largest single venue for such plants, together with the beds at the main entrance and the Dutch Garden, this would devastate the borough's primary planting showcase.

The Friends joined forces with a sister support group from the smaller Holland Garden, near Raynes Park, to campaign against the move, appealing both directly to the Council and via the local media for a change of direction.

The hotel too was severely shaken by a proposal that clearly threatened to undermine its setting for weddings and other functions. A special fund-raising dinner dance was held at Cannizaro House in cooperation with the Friends, raising £3000 at a stroke especially to help save the Sunken Garden. The campaign worked and Merton restored £100,000 to its annual parks budget, ensuring Cannizaro could relax for another year with its traditional displays of colour on show.

By the summer of 2005 a new level of co-operation seemed to have arrived with publication of the Merton Open Space Strategy, part of the London Mayor's plan for the future of open spaces throughout the capital. This included at last a commitment to increase frontline staffing in the parks after the years of decline. The sun appeared to have come out once more for Cannizaro Park, with the Friends and Merton not just talking but actually funding new planting jointly. The new upbeat spirit was complemented by the major artwork restorations of that year, the wonderful Zimbabwean sculpture show, return of the open air festival under a new three-year management deal, and a start at last of the grant application process to the Heritage Lottery Fund.

The only shadow seemed to be a new dispute between the Friends and the hotel over the planned construction of an orangery covering virtually the entire back terrace of the building. This would have changed an aspect of Cannizaro House that had remained intact since the house was rebuilt in 1901. Effective loss of the terrace threatened to separate the hotel and the park itself. The Friends were resolutely against it but the plan was first amended and then postponed for cost reasons.

In 2006 Merton Council saw a change of party control. As the Friends celebrated their tenth anniversary, a comprehensive five-year management plan was drawn up for Cannizaro Park. In August, the Committee met Lyn Carpenter, Merton's new head of Property and Leisure, and other officials. They heard that £548,000 was available for improvements in the borough's parks and although no further figures were given for Cannizaro in particular, the five-year plan would provide flexibility to respond to annual fluctuations in the maintenance spend. Services such as lawn mowing might be reduced to allow for other spending.

The Friends agreed to work closely with Merton on grant applications for several specific capital projects. A list of possible donor agencies was circulated and the Council was said to be committed to completing upgrades not just of the Aviary but also the main entrance and the Dutch Garden that year, while from April 2007 the Italian Garden would become a long-term priority. As the cost of completing this large area would require a substantial grant, the Friends would work in the meantime on securing funding for smaller projects including replacement of the park's broken fencing.

The last was largely in response to the continuing problem of overnight vandalism in the park. Despite the locked gates, intruders breaking through fences always brought damage and disturbance each summer. Worst of all had been a disastrous attack on the first Zimbabwean sculpture exhibition the previous year which had nearly ended the show at the start. The organiser had only decided to stay after receiving strong support from the Friends and the local community. Thankfully there were other exhibits to replace those destroyed and the show would go ahead to become a great success, repeated in two subsequent years. But the incident showed Cannizaro's vulnerability without adequate security.

Security apart, the other priority for the Friends was planting. This would have to take into account long-term changes in soil and irrigation conditions because of climate change. The Friends accepted Merton's argument that traditional annual bedding plants at the park's main entrance and in the Dutch Garden were not sustainable in the long term and could be sensibly replaced by herbs and more permanent hardy shrubs. However as a flagship display the Sunken Garden would be retained.

But within months it became clear what the relationship between the Friends and Merton actually amounted to. With no consultation, the new Council suddenly revived its predecessor's axe on all bedding plants and slashed £60,000 off the parks budget. The management plan for Cannizaro Park so laboriously put together with help from the Friends was set aside. Cannizaro's flagship status was scrapped along with that of Wimbledon Park, the borough's other Grade II* registered garden, and two other Grade II registered parks.

In April 2007, a second fund-raising dinner dance was organised by the Friends at Cannizaro House. It raised £4000 for the Sunken Garden, the borough's costliest bedding project. The Friends negotiated a compromise with Merton, paying for some planting themselves while the Council planted the lower eight beds. This saved a little spring colour.

But in June, Merton delivered another blow. Cooperation on the Heritage Lottery funding application, all that remained of the recent management plan, was rejected out of hand. That summer saw no bedding plants in Cannizaro Park or elsewhere in Merton. Disappointed visitors to the gardens saw bare beds for the first time in decades and the Friends were left appealing for voluntary donations to salvage the future.

They picked up the pieces, concentrating first on low key social activities for group members, prioritising tours, lectures and dinner dances while gradually improving morale. Two crucial figures were brought on to the scene in spring 2008: Anthony Gardiner, the herb specialist, and Sue White, a garden designer. Hired by the Friends to deal with the Dutch Garden and the beds at the park's main entrance respectively, each filled the void left by Merton's withdrawal of traditional bedding plants.

Anthony worked with the gardeners to plant 45 herb species in the Dutch Garden, converting it into a totally new feature, the Herb Garden. What had always been a "secret garden" to many visitors became an even more magical part of the park where a multiplicity of scents came to equal the visual in importance, among them thyme, sage, marjoram, feverfew, St John's wort, evening primrose and Roman chamomile.

Sue, meanwhile, designed beds between the main entrance and the Millennium Fountain to introduce topiary yews, hedges of *Sarcococca confusa*, blue and white *Vinca* types and a low growing *Euonymus*, a type of Spindle plant. No longer the garish colours seen during the last days of annual bedding, this became a gentle, permanent display, beckoning visitors beyond the noticeboards to enjoy Cannizaro's beauty and all it had to offer.

The gardening staff planted new birches opposite the Aviary, complementing the crocuses in winter and early spring. Using funds provided by the Friends, they were also able to plant *Polyanthus* to encourage a slow return to seasonal colour. It was a new start and Sue's additional design work later on for the beds beyond the hotel terrace marked a further return to cooperation with Merton. The Sunken Garden too was replanted to its former splendour in 2008 although long-term replacement of bedding plants by shrubs on its upper terraces would inevitably alter it in time.

In 2009 the Friends paid for three new signposts at strategic points in the park and a local couple donated the cost of two stylish wooden benches in the new Herb Garden. Carved with the maxim "Always together...never far apart" the benches represented the feelings of all those who loved Cannizaro Park, whatever their priorities for the gardens.

This was also a new era of cooperation between the park's gardening staff and volunteer pupils from the nearby King's College School. The boys' hard labour, given freely every Friday afternoon during the 2008-9 school terms, was able to achieve what the gardeners simply could not do alone in their limited hours at Cannizaro. They transformed many areas of the park, opening up new vistas, planting new rhododendrons, and restoring access to badly neglected areas of the Mediterranean Garden and Retreat. One additional gardener, borrowed temporarily from elsewhere in the borough, also made a great difference in those months.

In summer 2009 Chris Mountford became the sixth Chairman of the Friends of Cannizaro Park. Now retired from Merton Council, he was free to work directly on behalf of the Friends for the future of the park. No-one knew more about the gardens or the full story of the Friends since their foundation. In a sense the group had come full circle. For 13 years the Friends had been battling to protect and enhance these magnificent gardens. Their initiatives had benefited everyone with a love of the park and their achievements had been considerable.

Early in 2009, Gerard Hanberry, an Irish poet who had visited Cannizaro during a time of great personal emotion, sent a book of his work[2] to the Friends as an expression of thanks. His poem "In Cannizaro Park" said much about the timeless magic of the place in just a few words:

South London, a working Monday,
nobody about this concealed park,
only a trembling fragility of light and insects,
the musky scent of earth and sap. So silent, the great
metropolis seemed very far way.

NOTES

1. *Memories of My Side of the Common*, C Curry, 1988
2. *At Grattan Road*, G Hanberry, Salmon Poetry, 2009

*New signposts around the park (2009)*

# Chapter 8: The future

In 2009, English Heritage published its first ever list of historic registered parks and gardens considered to be at risk from neglect or development. Of 148 in London alone, no fewer than 14 (9.5%) were threatened. Only a small minority of the 148 shared Cannizaro's higher Grade II* status and 77.4% of those that did were not considered at any risk. Cannizaro Park, unmentioned, was among these.

No-one can really foretell the future for the estate that was once home to Dukes and Duchesses, statesmen, governors and magnates but has provided a magical retreat for anyone over the last 60 years. Merton, a London borough with widely diverging social needs and attitudes, shows little sign of increasing the manpower really needed to maintain the gardens at the standard they enjoyed in the early days of public ownership or in the planting heyday of the Wilsons. Yet English Heritage shows no apparent concerns about the park's continuing prospects as a Grade II* garden either.

In reality Cannizaro Park's future looks increasingly likely to depend on the Friends' effectiveness in raising voluntary support and donations. Their record since 1996 has been very good. Grant-giving bodies like the Heritage Lottery Fund may assist on specific capital projects and this is where the Friends will probably look in order to secure a major improvement to the Italian Garden in the next few years, a stated objective.

It will also depend on close cooperation with Merton Council, which recently secured substantial grants for other parks in the borough. However, the criteria included easily demonstrated social benefits such as better access for the disabled or improved play areas for children. To move forward, design and placement of facilities for Cannizaro Parkwill need to be in line with the requirements and expectations of the community and users of the park. It will need imagination and commitment in the years ahead.

Cannizaro's future as a venue for entertainment seems equally uncertain. The annual festival might return in favourable economic circumstances but future organisers will have to overcome the challenges of matching profitability to costs. Nevertheless the will is there and the arrival of yet another event management company in 2010, BSL, announcing the return of the festival showed it. Even the summer of 2009 did see an independent theatre company staging its own small-scale drama production in the park, "Man in the Iron Mask". Open air, low cost and with minimal props, it showed how effectively Cannizaro could still lure such artists to its magical setting.

After 30 years, Wimbledon College of Art still looks to Cannizaro to provide the annual setting for its now brief extravaganza of conceptual art. Monumental sculptures no longer bestride the lawns for weeks at a time (slowly succumbing to vandals), but art for its own sake shows an infinite capacity to adapt, using the park's bowers and swards to express the ideas of a fresh generation of students each spring.

Cannizaro's own community of artists in the studios includes painters, potters, sculptors and others who see it as a base from which to reach out to the wider world, reflecting the park itself in their work or just enjoying its tranquillity.

Cannizaro House remains Wimbledon's most exclusive hotel, offering rooms, dinners, weddings, meetings or just a pleasant evening in the restaurant, bar or terrace. Externally at least it would still be recognisable to those who knew it long ago.

Cannizaro's fourth century is just beginning. Sixty years of public ownership have brought new features. The Water Garden, Herb Garden, Azalea Dell, even the Sunken Garden, were all unknown when the Duke and Duchess of Cannizzaro tormented each other or the Drax family collected the ground rent. Changing climate and variable resources may change some aspects of this finest of parks in the future but to anyone who has trodden its paths and explored its hidden treasures, it will remain the magical retreat that has drawn so many to its gates for so long.

**TREES TO LOOK FOR**

Near the Aviary and Cannizaro House:
Atlantic Cedar *(Cedrus atlantica)*
Oriental plane *(Platanus orientalis)*
Magnolia *(Magnolia delavayi)*

Down the path towards the pond:
Brewer's Weeping Spruce *(Pica breweriana)*
Shagbark Hickory *(Carya ovata)*
Swamp Cypress *(Taxodium distichum)*.

Kitchen Garden:
Olive trees
Glory Tree *(Clerodendrum trichotomum)*,

Italian Garden:
Blue-berried mahonia
Swamp Cypresses
Sweet buckeye *(Aesculus flava)*

Wild Garden:
Snowdrop Tree *(Halesia carolina)*

Across stone bridge:
Berlin Poplar *(Populus berolinensis)*
Firs (red trunks)

Lady Jane's Wood:
Black Pine *(Pinus nigra)*
Common Oak *(Quercus robur)*

Mediterranean Garden:
Black Pine *(Pinus nigra)*
Pagoda Tree *(Sophora japonica)*

Near Azalea Tunnel:
Indian Horsechestnut *(Aesculus indica)*

Main lawns:
Three limes

Beyond Connoisseurs Corner:
Cork oak *(Quercus suber)*
Holm Oak

Beside Sunken Garden:
*Magnolia acuinata* (1949)

Beside Herb garden:
Acacias

Keir Garden:
*Eucalyptus dalrympleana*
Golden-rain tree *(Koelreuteria paniculata)*

Near allotments:
Cedar *(Cedrus Atlantica)*

Edge of lawn:
Roble beech *(Northofagus obliqua)*
Caucasian Wing Nut *(Pterocarya fraxinfolia)*

## RECORDED OCCUPANTS OF WARREN HOUSE 1710-1830 AND CANNIZARO HOUSE SINCE 1830

| | |
|---|---|
| William Browne | 1705-1738 |
| Thomas Walker | 1738-1748 |
| Stephen Skynner (not resident) | 1748-1749 |
| Thomas Grosvenor (not resident) | 1749-175? |
| Sir Benjamin Keene | 1755-1757 |
| Lyde Browne | 1757-1785 |
| Henry Dundas, Viscount Melville | 1787-1806 |
| Earl of Aberdeen | 1806-1807 |
| Sir Thomas Baring | 18??-1810 |
| Lord Lovaine | 18??-1812 |
| Sir James Sibbald | 1812-18?? |
| Duke and Duchess of Cannizzaro | 1817-1841 |
| Arthur Eden | 1842-1854 |
| Maharajah Duleep Singh | 1854-1854 |
| Vacant | 1854-1860 |
| John Boustead | 1860-1879 |
| Mary Schuster | 1879-1896 |
| Col Thomas Mitchell | 1896-1904 |
| Earl of Mexborough | 1904-1916 |
| American Red Cross Hospital | 1917-1918 |
| Percy Chubb | 1918-1919 |
| Edward Kenneth Wilson | 1920-1947 |
| Surrey County Council (Home/Elderly) | 1948-1977 |
| Vacant/Merton Arts | 1977-1987 |
| Thistle Hotels | 1987-2007 |
| Bridgehouse Hotels | 2007- |

# INDEX

Aberdeen, Earl of 35
ACAVA 67, 73, 92
Allison, Richard 43, 52, 62
Allison, William 42, 43
Almack's Assembly Room 8, 13-14
Ambassador Theatre Group 77-78

Beau Brummell 14
Bergami, Bartolommeo 14
Berry, James 89-90, 111
Bickford, A L 51-52
Black, Sir Cyril 66
Bonaparte, Lucien 23, 30
Borough Council, Merton 5, 61-67, 75-82, 87, 89-90, 92-100, 102
Borough Council, Wimbledon 7, 39, 41, 44, 47, 49-53, 56, 57
Boustead, John 8, 36, 106
Bridgehouse Hotels 67, 106
Brown, Lancelot "Capability" 31, 42
Browne, Lyde 32-33, 64, 106
Browne, William 31, 42, 106

Cambridge, Duke of 20, 28
Cannizaro Trust 66
Cannizaro, Duke of (See Platamone, Francis)
Cannizaro, Duchess of (See Johnstone, Sophia)
Cartagenova (Di Novo) 25-27
Cecil, Sir Thomas 31
Christian, Toby 73, 93
Chubb, Percy 40-41

Dee, Charlotte 17
De Mazenod, Eugene, Bishop of Marseilles 13
Dillistone, George 42-43
Dino, Duchess of 13-14, 23, 30

Disraeli, Benjamin 8, 11
Drakeford, Tony 89, 91, 111
Drax family 3, 40-41, 48, 103
Drax, Sir Reginald 40-41, 49-50, 52, 54
Dundas, Henry, Viscount Melville 17, 33-35, 42-43, 48, 106
Dutch Garden 44, 58, 96, 98-99

English Heritage 5, 43, 62-63, 65, 67, 77, 102
Esterhazy 14, 18-19, 22

Fawcett, Patrick 7, 11, 111
Fison, Peter 91
Fitzherbert, Mrs 18, 22
Ford, Martha 16-18

Gardiner, Anthony 82, 90, 99
Greville, Charles 13-15, 21, 24-25, 27, 30
Griffiths, Jon 68, 74
Grosvenor family 32, 40, 106
Guides, Girl 7, 44

Haile Selassie, Emperor 45-46, 67, 81-82, 93-94
Hamlin, Alderman W E 7, 10
Hanberry, Gerard 100, 111
Hastings, Eveline 2, 82, 87, 95
Heritage Lottery Fund 95, 97-98, 102
Holman, Martin 89, 111
Hopper, Henry 56, 58-59
Hore-Belisha, Leslie 41

Italian Garden 32, 62, 74-76, 78, 87, 92, 95, 98, 102, 104

John Evelyn Society (Wimbledon Society) 2, 35, 41, 62, 65-66, 80, 89, 111-112
Johnstone, Alexander Patrick 16, 18
Johnstone, Emily 18-20, 28
Johnstone, Commodore George 2, 15-17, 29-30, 33-34

Johnstone, George Bueller  18, 28
Johnstone, George Lindsay  16-18
Johnstone, James Primrose  16, 18
Johnstone, John Lowther, Baronet of Westerhall  17-18
Johnstone, Sophia, Duchess of Cannizzaro  2, 12, 14-30, 33, 35, 37, 47, 65, 67, 103, 106

Kauffmann, Angelica  65
Kew Gardens  7, 10, 28, 49-50, 54, 58, 91
Keir, The  44-45, 48, 52, 58, 92, 105
King George III  15, 34
King's College School  96, 100
Kitchen Garden  32, 43, 49, 53, 55, 58, 60-62, 67, 78, 92, 104

Lady Jane's Wood  33, 42-43, 60, 95, 104
Lofthouse, Dave  87, 90-92
Lyas, Michael  76-77, 111

Matthews, Tony  2, 94 (pictured), 111
Mexborough, John Savile, Earl of  39-40, 42, 106
Mitchell, Colonel Thomas  37-38, 44, 48, 106
Mountford, Chris  82, 90-92, 100, 111
Munster, Hilary, Countess of  44, 47, 48-50
Munster, Earl of  47

Neave, Edwin M  50-52
Neumann, Baron Philip von  18-22, 27-30, 67
Newth, Martin  2, 68, 74

Opera Box  77

Pickering, W J  53
Pitt, William  33-35
Platamone, Baldassarre, Duke of Cannizzaro  12-13, 22
Platamone, Concetta, the Contessa  12-13, 28
Platamone, Francis, Duke of Cannizzaro  12-30, 103, 106
Platamone, Michele, Prince Ludica  12-13, 22, 28

PMB Holdings 78
Prince Regent (King George IV) 13-14, 20, 22

Queen Victoria 26, 28, 52

Raikes, Thomas 23, 28, 30
Robert Holmes & Co 76, 78, 111
Rome, Richard 68, 90
Rosalia, Princess Ladaria 12
Rose Garden 58
Royal Wimbledon Golf Course 9, 32, 41, 45, 50-51, 54

Saint Antonio, George Wellington Francis Balthasar 14
Schuster, Adela 36-37
Schuster, Mary 36-37, 44, 47, 106
Select Committee on Public Works 7
Seligman, Hilda 45-46, 93
Seligman, Nancy-Joan 93-94, 111
Singh, Maharajah Duleep 36, 106
Spencer, Earl 31
Sunken Garden 7, 35, 43, 59, 81, 88, 92, 96-99, 103, 105

Tennyson, Alfred Lord 36-37
Thistle Hotels 66, 88, 106
Visconti, Madame 21, 23, 25

Walker, Cyril 53-54
Walker, Thomas 31, 106
Walpole, Horace 32
Warren Farm 9, 32, 41
Wellington, Duke of 14, 20, 22-23, 26, 30
White, Sue 99
Wilberforce, William 35, 65
Wilde, Oscar 36, 48
Williamson, Robert 77
Wilson, Edward Kenneth 41, 43-44, 46, 52, 65, 106
Wimbledon School (College) of Art 35, 67-68, 73, 81, 87, 90, 92-93, 103
Wimbledon Society (See John Evelyn Society)

Zimbabwean sculptures 74-75, 90, 97-98

# ACKNOWLEDGEMENTS

The author would especially like to thank Charles Toase, chairman of the Wimbledon Society Local History Group, for his assistance in compiling much of the historical material in this book. Many thanks also to Deborah Bauer, Peter Beckwith, John Collard, Betty Dobson, Gerard Hanberry, Martin Holman, Robert Holmes, Janie Jeffries, Michael Lyas, Ann McAllister, Chris Mountford, Dennis Robbins and Nancy-Joan Seligman.
Further thanks to James Berry, Tony Drakeford, and the late Richard Milward, William Myson, Henry Hopper, Patrick Fawcett and Constance Curry whose earlier work also made this possible.

## Chairs of the Friends of Cannizaro Park

Eveline Hastings 1996-2000
Alan Gingell 2000-2002
Sarah Newton 2002-2004
Tony Matthews 2004-2007
Juliet Willis 2007-2009
Chris Mountford 2009-

# MUSEUM OF WIMBLEDON

## THE WIMBLEDON SOCIETY
## MUSEUM OF LOCAL HISTORY
website www.wimbledonmuseum.org.uk

The Museum of Wimbledon is run by the registered charity, The Wimbledon Society, and is on the corner of Ridgway and Lingfield Road in Wimbledon. It is open on Saturdays and Sundays between 2:30 and 5:00 pm or at other times by arrangement. For information please telephone 020 8296 9914. Our staff will gladly help you with your questions about local history. Alternatively take a look at our website www.wimbledonmuseum.org.uk where you can see our collections, buy books and contact us with your queries or comments.

Buses 93 and 200 pass close by. There is only limited parking in local side streets. Wheelchair access is unfortunately not possible.

If you like Wimbledon, as a resident or visitor, you'll enjoy it even more when you know something of its fascinating history. We'll be glad to welcome you to our place and show you the past. There is a wide selection of books and pamphlets about Wimbledon and the surrounding areas, together with maps and a fully-digitised collection of over 2,000 paintings, drawings and photographs. Entry is free.

Museum of Wimbledon, 22 Ridgway, Wimbledon, London SW19 4QN
email: wimbledonmuseum@yahoo.co.uk

The Wimbledon Society
Registered Charity No. 269478